I LOVE PRAYER

I ♥ PRAYER

Connected to God, Changing the World

by Rachel Hickson

HEARTCRY
FOR CHANGE

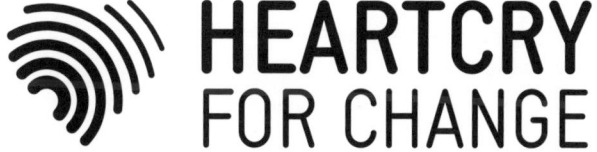

Produced by Heartcry for Change
www.heartcryforchange.com

A Publication by Heartcry Ministries
PO Box 737 I Oxford I Oxon I OX1 9FA I UK

www.heartcryforchange.com

Heartcry Ministries UK Registered Charity 1076993

ISBN: 978-0-9837641-5-1

I Love Prayer
Connected to God, Changing the World
by Rachel Hickson

Book cover and content layout designed by David Hickson

Edited by the Heartcry Team

Printed and bound in the UK by **Speed Agency** – Elton, Peterborough

Second Edition – Printed August 2018

Dedication

I love prayer but I have also discovered the joy of grandchildren!

At the time of writing this book I have 5 wonderful grandkids and would love to dedicate this book to them – a legacy that brings me great joy.

Leila
Just keep talking to Jesus and He will share great secrets with you.

Cooper
Enjoy all the excitement of adventures with Jesus.

Elani
You will always be God's special princess.

Annabelle
Jesus will be able to answer all your "tricky" questions.

Jeremy
You already carry such peace and the joy of God.

Acknowledgements

This part of the book is impossible to write!

How can you express your gratitude to each person who deserves it?

I am sure I will forget someone – so thank you!

But I do want to thank my husband, **Gordon**, you are such a great encourager!

I want to thank **Helen Azer**, my friend and colleague. She is an incredible person, theologically trained, who loves reading complicated texts and doing research, and without her this book would have been much more difficult to write.

I also want to thank an army of volunteers, and especially **Pauline Azer**, who have read the manuscript, helped correct my grammar, spotted repetition errors, advised me on the theology and content, and given me hope. Thank you for all your reading time!

Finally thank *you* for buying this book.

I hope that it will be more than just another book but that it will inspire you to be a person of prayer who changes the world around you!

So now ENJOY and be ready to change!

Contents

Foreword

It has been said that prayer is the world's greatest wireless connection. For me that's both good and bad news: wifi gives me incredible access to an infinitely exciting wealth of communication opportunities as well as the possibility to explore new horizons. But there is the small matter of needing a consistently good connection to stay online if I really want to download all that is accessible to me. Unfortunately, all too frequently, the wifi connection leaves much to be desired! If we're honest, most of us have a similar love/hate relationship with prayer too: it offers us the great privilege of supernatural communication with God but, at times, we feel our "connection" is intermittent or frustratingly lacking. We can lose confidence in our ability to pray altogether and tend to ask others to pray for us instead, believing that their prayer will break through where ours has apparently failed to yield results. But Rachel is a cheerleader whose greatest joy is to see people connected to God and equipped to change their world, and she knows that a vibrant, personal prayer life is the key for each of us. So this book is a tool to help you get online again!

I Love Prayer – Connected to God, Changing the World will take you on an adventure to rediscover your passion for prayer and encourage you to explore new territory that will make you more hungry for God and more compassionate towards people. This book will also stretch your capacity and equip you with revelation and understanding into why it is that the Church must arise with a new and radical conviction that Jesus really is the only hope for our nations. As His Bride, we have been given royal authority to let our prayers be the fulcrum which tips our communities into the goodness of God and brings change.

Nowhere illustrates this more profoundly than praying in a capital city. As I have discovered on numerous prayer assignments in recent years, capital cities have an atmosphere all of their own. It is in a capital city where you become more acutely aware of how all the contradictions, challenges and prophetic potential of a nation collide. Here they are amplified and focussed, like rays of sun through a magnifying glass, until they ignite a fire. Only a revelation of the battle which rages for them, and the nations they represent, can explain why our nations' capital cities are such contested spiritual ground. Being part of intercessory prayer teams, I have learned that it is the role, and privilege, of the Church to ensure that capital cities burn with revival fire and reformation, rather than the destructive inferno of an enemy who delights to derail the plans of God for a nation by bringing natural and spiritual government out of alignment. This book explains how the principles of staking the ground and developing the practice of prayer walking can release healing and restoration to the land so that our communities can get reconnected to God's original design and purpose for them.

Most of us have prophetic words over our lives, communities and nations. If you want to learn how to engage with these words and activate their full potential, then this book is for you! Rachel's disarming writing style, and countless stories of how prayer really does work, will encourage you to break out of every limitation and begin a new journey of faith that will enable you to say, with integrity, "I Love Prayer"!

HELEN AZER

Introduction and Comment

There is a new hunger in the world – a fresh desire to know God. There is a new sound vibrating in the nations. Can you hear the sound of passionate, praying people? People who want to have a meaningful relationship and live a life connected to God. People who want to pray.

Frequently, after I have finished speaking at a conference, people approach me asking, "Please will you train us? Can you mentor me?" I have often wondered why they ask me this question as there are so many people who are better qualified. But one day someone explained this request further: "Rachel, when you talk we can see you love Jesus and I want to know how to connect with Him. I want to learn to talk to God. I want it to be real!" Challenged by this observation I have written this book. We can sense that these are urgent times and we need to pray effectively but we must also enjoy the journey. I really believe that the Holy Spirit wants to tutor you in His school of prayer, because God longs for you to connect with Him as never before.

Today God is looking for an army of ordinary people who will do extraordinary things. This is not a time for us to stand back and feel that only the spiritual "superstars" can take the lead, but this is a new day for ordinary men, women, grandparents, youth and children to go to the place of prayer together and change their world. These are exciting days! God wants each of us to build houses of prayer wherever we live so that we begin to see a radical transformation in the spiritual atmosphere of our neighbourhoods, our cities, and our nations. It is time for each one of us to arise and take our responsibility. These are urgent days and we need all hands on deck.

All over the world, prayer is taking a higher priority in people's lives than ever before. These days it is not uncommon for people to take time off from work in order to spend a day in focussed prayer. In the past this would have been unheard of. In fact, even if you had offered to pay people to go to a church prayer meeting, they probably would have chosen to stay at home! But God is doing a new thing to raise the profile of prayer. All over the world there is a divine heartbeat – a call to prayer that is becoming so strong: "Come on Church, now is the time to pray!" My prayer is that God will use this teaching to prepare your heart and to call you to a new place of dedicated prayer.

RACHEL HICKSON

1 I am a Friend of God

THE PRIVILEGE OF PRAYER

I love prayer because my Mum infected me with her passion for prayer. I remember as a little girl after Mum put me to bed and tucked me up, she would kneel by my bed with her face close to mine, and we would pray. I would sense her heart of prayer and feel the breath of her words across my cheeks and I knew God was listening. She taught me to pray by showing me her love for Jesus. A love for prayer is infectious and we need to be captivated by this privilege of connecting with and talking to God.

Just reading a book will not teach you to pray. Learning to pray is more about developing your relationship than your technique. We need to be inspired to pray. We need to be ready to sacrifice and make time to pray. We need to be motivated by a hunger to know Jesus more. When you meet individuals who are passionate about prayer you will discover that they are passionate about Jesus too. When people begin to see this authentic prayer modelled, they begin to long for it. So much of prayer is caught and not taught. As leaders we need to be those who provoke and provide people with an environment where they can experience true prayer and get hungry for God. After a time of prayer people should respond and say, "Wow! I want to learn to pray like that; I've seen *you* pray and now *I* want to have my own connection with God."

This is what happened when the disciples watched Jesus pray. They were captivated by His relationship with the Father and they wanted to learn to pray. In Luke 11:1 we read this account:

> *"One day Jesus was praying in a certain place. When he finished one of his disciples said to Him, 'Lord, teach us to pray, just as John taught His disciples.'"*

When I think of Jesus and all the incredible things He did: raising the dead, healing the blind, silencing the storm, changing water into wine – I wonder what I would choose to learn from Jesus. If we were given the opportunity to have a personal tutorial with Jesus, what would we ask for? It is interesting that Jesus' disciples, who lived with Him and often saw Him moving in the supernatural, never asked Him, "Lord, teach us how to do miracles." They cried out, "Lord, teach us to pray!" I believe this cry is stirring in God's people all over the world right now. People are saying, just like the disciples did, "Oh Jesus, please teach me to pray." We are making a great choice. As we pursue God and love Him with our hearts we need to realize the responsibility and privilege we have of showing people how to pray. Like Jesus, we need to teach and inspire others to pray; and so we need to let them watch us in the place of prayer.

RUINED REPUTATION REDEEMED

Prayer is changing and is no longer boring! Unfortunately, many of us who have been brought up in church remember prayer meetings as a tedious ordeal needing to be endured and rarely enjoyed. We remember those terrible sessions where people prayed long, irrelevant prayers, and we struggled to keep awake. But this is a new day and prayer is redeeming its ruined reputation. All over the world people are discovering that prayer is an exciting and stimulating experience.

Often we have wanted to avoid this topic of prayer as it makes us feel guilty. Somehow we have believed a lie that everyone else prays more effectively and regularly than we do. We have allowed our sense of consistent failure to convince us we are inadequate and let these thoughts rob our desire to pray. At other times we have prayed and prayed but nothing has happened or, if anything, things have got worse. This has just compounded our feelings of disappointment and unfulfilled hopes and so we have withdrawn from a life of prayer. Yet in the midst of all these negative thoughts we can hear the call of God which stirs the desire to pray. If this is you, let God renew your expectation and help you eradicate all those negative memories.

UNIQUE SOUNDS OF PRAYER

There is no perfect way to pray. But there is a right way for you to connect with God in this season of your life. As we begin to commit our lives to prayer, we must recognize that the way in which each of us communicates is so individual. There is no generic model of prayer that will fit everyone. Each person must discover the style of prayer that is uniquely *their* expression. Some people are very loud and demonstrative during their prayer time while others are more meditative and enjoy the pregnant silence of contemplative prayer. Neither way is right or wrong – but together these cries make a symphony of perfect prayer calling from our communities and cities.

Each one of us must embark on our own prayer journey and intentionally find our distinct sound. We need to learn how to connect and relate to God. We need to develop our own love language and talk to God and learn to listen. However, whatever our personality there will inevitably be seasons where we will be more demonstrative or silent. Even the quietest person does shout when provoked. Just try to kidnap their child. They will yell to attract attention and they will not stop shouting until you release their kid! In the same way, in the place of prayer, there are seasons when God stirs a warrior cry within us and we shout at the enemy who is robbing and stealing from our lives. There are other times when we need to rest in the presence of God and just be still. It is not a time for words but waiting and listening. Allow God to teach you the right sound for this season.

HOW LONG IS A "REAL" PRAYER TIME?

How much time should I spend in prayer to have a "proper" prayer life? In our eagerness to please God we often ask the wrong questions. If we define prayer as being our genuine communication connection with God then surely we never want to be offline! We need to understand that prayer is not just about defined times of cognitive conversation but also about an attitude of consistent connection. Stay online – keep connected!

We are all familiar with using the internet these days and understand that although we can be online 24/7 there are only definite times when we are actively dialoguing. The moment you hear that "ping" you know you have received a message and you get ready to engage. In the same way we need to develop an expectation that God may speak at any time and we need to be ready to talk with Him.

However, you will also need to grasp times to just focus and pray. Your prayer life will have different seasons and you need to develop a healthy rhythm of prayer for this period of your life. For instance, when you have a young baby, you are up in the night, your sleep will be disturbed, and your life is demanding so you do well if you are able to snatch five minutes here and there in which to pray. Maybe you previously had a season where you were able to pray regularly for two hours a day, but, now you have a young child, you are grabbing time whenever you can. You are doing well to take those five minutes – this is just a different season so be kind to yourself. So many young mums come to me depressed about this. "I think I'm backsliding", they say. I say to them, "Sweetie, if you are managing to pray at all as well as feeding your baby and doing all the other things that need doing, then you are doing an amazing job!"

Do not be too hard on yourself. Prayer is not filling in a time sheet and ticking some boxes to pass a test with God. Prayer is enjoying being a child of our Father. So, simply ask the Holy Spirit, "Lord, teach me to pray in this season." As your life changes, allow your patterns of prayer to change too. So how do we develop a consistent personal prayer life? I would like to give you a few basic building blocks that can form a healthy foundation for an effective and fulfilling prayer life:

DUTY OR DELIGHT?

To have a happy prayer life you need a deep revelation that prayer is all about relationship. You need to delight in this opportunity to be a friend of God. If it becomes a duty or just "another 'to do' task in my busy life", then you have forgotten the privilege of being connected with God. We must eradicate the idea that prayer is just *another meeting* that we have to attend. Prayer is much more about intimacy with God. It is more about being with God than doing things for Him.

All around the world the advertising companies are telling us to upgrade to higher speed internet connections. So, as we desire to see God's power poured out in signs, wonders and miracles, we need to upgrade our life connection to God and then watch His power being downloaded from Heaven to earth through us as we pray.

PARTNERS TOGETHER

No one is able to construct an effective prayer life without the help of the Holy Spirit. We need to work in partnership with Him as we pray. In Romans 8:26 we read about this partnership:

> *"Likewise the Spirit helps us in our weakness. For we do not know what to pray for as we ought, but the Spirit himself intercedes for us with groanings too deep for words." (ESV)*

So let us look at this scripture line by line and learn the secret of this partnership.

> "In the same way, the Spirit helps us in our weakness."

I find it so comforting that when the Bible is talking about prayer, God immediately says, "Don't worry! I know this is an area of weakness for you." God knows exactly where our natural nature struggles and provides us with a perfect life coach. Anyone who feels that good prayer is impossible for them should be encouraged, because the Holy Spirit is aware of what you need. In fact, God goes further and says to us, "That is *why* I've given you the Holy Spirit. He is there for you in your weakness." So press into this supernatural partnership and enjoy your times of prayer.

NOT KNOWING WHAT TO PRAY

Many of us draw back from the place of prayer as we feel our words are pointless or lack true fluency. We feel inadequate as we do not know how to tackle life's emergencies: we suddenly feel tongue tied and become convinced we are not praying correctly for such a critical need. Most of us know that we should pray and even want to pray about these important situations and yet we fear we cannot find the right words. But God reassures us as Romans 8:26 continues:

> "In the same way, the Spirit helps us in our weakness. We do not know what we ought to pray for, but the Spirit himself intercedes for us with groans that words cannot express."

Usually when we receive a prayer request we initially respond by wanting to pray for the urgent situation, but can then feel we have no idea how to pray to guarantee that our prayer brings a change into these circumstances. But God has an answer and that is the Spirit Himself – not a substitute, but the Holy Spirit Himself will intercede with us. Isn't that incredible! We need to have a revelation that the Holy

Spirit desires our obedience more than our expertise in prayer. This prayer partnership is far more than mere words. Prayer is something supernatural! Every time we make that decision to connect with the Holy Spirit in the place of prayer, something supernatural happens that is beyond us. Although we feel weak and we do not know how to articulate our prayers, the Spirit Himself comes alongside us.

Imagine for a moment standing side by side with a friend so that your shoulders are touching. This is the image that Paul is seeking to convey to us: that when the Spirit comes alongside you, you stand *shoulder to shoulder*. When that happens, it's not just about "me" anymore, it's about *us being yoked together*. Our shoulders are now jointly carrying the burden in the place of prayer. Where I am weak, He is strong; when I don't know what to pray for, He has perfect knowledge. Together we can break through!

Every time you pray, I want you to use this picture: you are a *prayer team*, working together with the Holy Spirit. Prayer is not about you alone on earth, desperately trying to reach a big God "somewhere up in the sky". A more accurate picture is you working alongside the Holy Spirit as He helps connect you to Heaven. Every time you don't know how to pray, the *Spirit Himself* will complete your prayer. He will help you and direct you and enable you to have a successful prayer life.

However, if you think that now the Holy Spirit is helping you to pray, your prayers will suddenly sound so much more "professional" and impressive, think again! In this passage Paul reminds us that the Spirit will intercede through us with *groans that words cannot express*. We will discover that our English may sound less fluent but our spiritual language, the cry of our heart, will be expressed perfectly. I've discovered that the more I let the Holy Spirit into my prayer life, the more unpolished my prayers have sounded. As the Holy Spirit touches you with His revelation something deep is evoked from within that was not expressed before. A new cry, a new desperation, a new hunger is awakened. Tears are often expressed; your prayer may become emotional and not just factual. You begin to carry with God the prayer burden of the situation and feel it as you pray for it. This groaning with the Spirit in prayer is labouring and working spiritually. You may not even utter a word but those very tears are powerful words of prayer. Often you will just feel something deep being expressed within you that goes beyond the place of actual words – but that is prayer! Prayer is not about the sound you make, it is about your spirit being connected to God in an intimate conversation, and God is committed to help you learn this skill.

EYES CLOSED – TIME TO PRAY!

Often I think the tradition to close your eyes when you pray just helps you to fall asleep! Normal people tend to fight sleep rather than pray even in the midst of an emergency. Remember the story of the disciples in the Garden of Gethsemane from Mark 14:37. We can judge the disciples for their insensitivity, but if we are honest we have all had friends in a crisis who have asked us to pray and we have either forgotten or fallen asleep rather than pray for them.

In Gethsemane, when Jesus returned to His disciples and found them sleeping, he asked Peter, "Are you asleep?". I am sure Peter would have loved to reply, "No, no Lord, I was not sleeping. I was just meditating and in deep prayer!". But of course he was fast asleep! "Can't you watch with me for one hour?", Jesus asked Peter. What is the honest answer to that question? The truthful answer is, no, I am not very good at watching and praying even in a time of emergency. We have all discovered the reality of this statement that the spirit is willing but the flesh is *really* weak. It is God who transforms our spirits and puts His heart's cry within us, and gives us strength to press through in prayer. Indeed, most of us have a real *willingness* to pray, but so often our intentions do not follow through into action. This is where the tension occurs, when our choices fail to come into line with the inner desires of our spirit.

So how do we overcome this tension? Again God has provided an answer. We ask the Holy Spirit to train us in a new area of discipline "God, I want to pray, but I have to confess that my body is weak and I tend to sleep and forget to pray. Holy Spirit, please come alongside me and help me." Do not allow yourself to get depressed or condemned by your inability to pray. Your situation is not unusual. We all have to learn to conquer our natural prayerlessness and face the fact that we have a tendency to be sleepy and forget our promise to pray. But in this season let your fresh desire to pray motivate you into a new level of dependency on the Holy Spirit who will instruct you how to pray effectively.

THE DIVINE TRANSFORMER AND ADAPTOR

I spend my life travelling to different nations where I am often challenged by the fact that my electrical equipment will not fit into the different shaped power socket. What do I need? A travel plug adaptor. This is a perfect illustration of how the Holy Spirit comes alongside us to help connect us to Heaven as we pray. We have our expression and language but as we connect through the Holy Spirit to God He gives us divine help to adapt our language and help us break through. The Holy Spirit comes and takes my words, He takes who I am, and He adapts it to connect it with Almighty God. To express your prayer effectively, you must keep plugging into the Holy Spirit and let Him be your adaptor.

But sometimes you need more than an adaptor to get the powerful connection you require. You also need a transformer. Different nations have different voltage supplies. The Europeans have 240 volts while the Americans have a 110 volt supply. So, whenever I am in the USA, even though I'm using my adaptor to plug my hairdryer into the socket correctly, it still needs more power to work effectively. This is a good illustration of our prayer. As we begin to talk to God, our prayer can seem powerless. We can feel, "How can this prayer heal my friend with cancer? God, I need more power!" In this moment we need to let the Holy Spirit take our willing words and transform them into powerful weapons for the pulling down of strongholds. The Bible promises us that power is released when the Holy Spirit comes upon us. Jude encourages us to pray in the Holy Spirit: In Jude 1:20 we read:

> "But you, dear friends, build yourselves up in your most holy faith and pray in the Holy Spirit".

We need to learn to let the Holy Spirit adapt and empower our prayer life.

So let your prayer be connected to the adaptor and transformer of the Holy Spirit and become powerful. All the books you read and the seminars you attend can help *inform* you but it is *this connection* that is going to *transform* your prayer life.

BECOMING A FRIEND OF JESUS

Friendship will keep your passion for prayer alive. We need to become a friend of Jesus, as well as keeping the Holy Spirit alongside us when we pray. We need to develop a healthy two-way communication with God. We need to understand that prayer is more than a place to ask for help with our most recent crisis but also find a place of exchange and conversation. As someone once said, "Prayer is not about seeking an answer but about seeking the One who has all the power to answer!" We need to expect to hear God speaking with us. Prayer is about knowing that as you draw near to the heart of God, God is going to touch your life too.

The Bible is the account of the greatest romance, where God expresses His unending love for mankind. It is the true original love story where the bridegroom of Heaven, the royal Prince of all Princes, falls in love with a commoner and desires to make her the princess of Heaven, His royal bride. Eventually the day of the great wedding comes, the bride is beautifully prepared and ready, and they are perfectly united. Together they then live happily ever after in the presence of the almighty King of Kings! It is an incredible love story of epic proportions! It is into this journey of love that we are invited to come. God wants to be our friend.

WHERE IS MY FRIEND?

But let us pause for a moment and remember how this friendship was lost. At the beginning of this love story God created Adam and Eve and placed them in the beautiful Garden of Eden where he could walk and talk with them. God and man enjoyed wonderful times of fellowship, until one day everything changed as recorded in Genesis chapter 3. However, when we teach about the fall of man, we usually emphasize what *we* lost. We teach about how we fell into sin, how we lost our place in the Garden, how we lost our relationship with the Father. But as I was reading this passage one day, God spoke to me: "*Rachel, have you ever considered what I lost that day?*"

Have you ever stopped to think that God lost his friends when man sinned in the Garden? We are so focussed on our loss that we often never consider the agony to the heart of God. He lost his friendship with man. God and Adam often walked and talked together in the garden, enjoying one another's company. In Genesis 3:9 we read that God is walking once again in the Garden, looking for Adam. Having sinned, Adam and Eve hear God coming and hide from Him. So the Lord calls out, "Where are you?" Can you hear the anguish of that cry? Since I had this revelation, I no longer interpret or hear that cry as the sound of an angry parent looking for a lost child; but I hear a cry of grief as God realizes that He has lost His friend and the great sacrifice that will be needed to restore it. Since that day, God's cry has never changed. The Father is still calling mankind, "Where are you?" because we were created for relationship and communication with Him. This is why Jesus, the darling of Heaven, offered to lay His life down for the Father. Why? He did this because it was the only way that this communication gap could be restored again. The Father wanted the barrier of sin to be removed so that every man, woman and child could become connected to Him in a living relationship once again. The cry of God has always been friendship. He says, "I want to know you." From the least to the greatest He wants to know us. He wants a heart to heart transparent relationship and He is calling you to come.

AFRAID OF TRANSPARENCY

Truly transparent friendships are rare. Most of us hide something due to fear and a sense of inadequacy. We do not want to be judged and so we hide. When God calls Adam we read that he hid too.

> "But the Lord God called to the man, 'Where are you?' And he answered, 'I heard you were in the garden and I was afraid because I was naked and so I hid.'" (Genesis 3:9)

Here we see that fear will rob us of a real and open relationship with God. Adam's response to God's question reveals how he has allowed his fear to position him wrongly. In fact this is the first place that fear is mentioned in the Bible and it is linked to our communication with God. So often we allow fear to intimidate us and so become afraid to talk to God honestly. The enemy condemns us and we feel a sense of shame and so hide our true feelings. But God so desires to have an intimate communication with us and the devil will do everything he can to stop us connecting. God wants you to talk to Him, so the enemy constantly whispers to you, "Don't talk! Your prayers are pathetic. No one is going to listen to you. You're irrelevant. You can't say it right!" Yet, the cry of God has never changed: "Where are you? I want to talk with you." The enemy will use every kind of intimidation to silence our passion. His tactics have not changed since that first time in the garden. So we must come with a bold determination and say, "Father, I am going to break every shred of intimidation and fear off my life. I believe I can have an incredible relationship with you and I will hear your voice."

God is calling you to meet with Him face to face. I remember the first time Gordon, my husband, took me in his arms and kissed me. Before he kissed me he held my face in his hands and looked deeply into my eyes. I remember a sense of panic that wanted to push him away as I felt too vulnerable and overwhelmed by my sense of rejection. But Gordon understood this dilemma and just held me closer. Over the months as he held me I grew accustomed to this place and his face and I learned to love it. My fearful place has become my safe place and a place of healing. This is the kind of communication that God wants with you – looking into the depths of your being and being completely transparent. To feel comfortable in this place you need to carry a fresh revelation that God has completely delivered you from all your sin and shame. You need to know just how thoroughly and utterly God has forgiven you. When you believe that you are loved and clean you will walk with your head up and shoulders back into the presence of God, not with any sense of arrogance, but with the correct confidence of knowing you are loved by God. Your God welcomes your presence and you can look into the eyes of Jesus, your Bridegroom, and know His voice.

YOU BRING PLEASURE TO GOD

In the first chapter of the book of Song of Songs, the bride has a wrong picture of herself. She says, in effect, "Don't look at me. I'm dark... I'm ugly...I'm small-breasted..." But by the end of Song of Songs the consistent love of the Bridegroom has completely changed her perspective. She now sees herself in a new light and says, "I am full breasted and I bring him great contentment." Her identity has been healed by the love of God. But not only has the Bridegroom given her something, but she now knows she has something worthwhile to give too. Throughout the Bible the "breast" illustrates the place of provision and nourishment, and suddenly this bride realizes she is not as redundant as she thought but God has made her a resource of plenty.

We all need this revelation that we can bring pleasure to God. In response to the cry of God calling, "Where are you?", we can walk into His presence and say, "Father, here I am! I am here for you." Something rejoices in the heart of God when we do that. The very fact that we choose to take time to be in His presence brings Him joy. As you spend time with God He will share who He is with you too! You will find yourself having dreams, wisdom, revelations, prophetic words, as you spend time with Him. This is the natural outworking of a friendship with God – you become like Him.

BEING OR DOING?

I love the scripture John 15:15 that says:

> "I no longer call you servants, because a servant does not know his master's business. Instead, I have called you friends, for everything that I have learned from my Father I have made known to you."

One of the most difficult disciplines to learn is the practice of *being* with God and not just being busy *doing* for God! The relationship of a servant and friend are different as they have different levels of privilege and trust. Here the servant represents a relationship where you only expect a reward for the work you have done. You have a mind-set which only expects a blessing based entirely upon your ability to perform. You have done your duty, fulfilled your orders and now expect a reward. This is how a servant thinks. But God does not want us to be "human doings", He wants us to be "human beings", able to have a true relationship with Him and be His friend. We are called to approach God on an entirely different basis, knowing that He is a friend who longs to share His heart with us. God does not want to give you a job and then relate to you as the Boss but he wants to share the journey with you as a friend.

The second part of the scripture should impact us, *"Instead, I have called you friends, for everything that I have learned from my Father I have made known to you."* Isn't that incredible? This is the level of the friendship that God wants. Complete transparency. Jesus is saying that everything He has learned from His Father in that secret place He wants to share with us. That is a big download of information!

Good friendships take time. If you are prepared to put quality time into a relationship then you will be rewarded with a more intimate knowledge and understanding of that person. If you give time, then you will receive information. This same principle works in our friendship with God. If you will give Him your time He will share the secrets of Heaven with you and allow you to understand things that were previously hidden. There are many areas where the Church needs fresh insight and wisdom but these revelations will not be given to us unless we spend time talking with God.

We all understand that if we want to download large files from the Internet we have to remain online a longer time than if we are just checking a short message. In the same way, if you want to have access to greater depths of God then you need to take the time to listen and download this information. But will you carve time out of your day and make this happen? Praying time is never convenient but we need to just be obedient! So often we are just crisis friends, we only seek the face of God when our life is tough and we need help, but I believe that God wants us to be consistent friends that are available for Him even when we do not need an answer for our personal lives. We need to have a two-way friendship and become a faithful friend that enjoys talking with Him even when we feel fine!

DECISION TIME – BE A FRIEND OF GOD

Finally, as you acknowledge your desire to be a friend of God, remember that each person's call to prayer will have a different sound. Different people are called to pray for different areas of geography or places of influence. Some of us will identify more readily with our neighbourhoods, while others will feel compelled to pray for particular nations; many of us feel we have enough to pray for within our own families! So do not push yourself to pray into too many areas; just come and talk to God and be His friend. Just as friends love to talk about different things and areas of interest, we need to acknowledge that some people are called to pray for missions, while others pray for individual needs. So ask God to show you what He wants to talk to you about and let Him direct your conversations with Heaven.

IDENTIFY YOUR PRAYER SEASONS

Even as you begin to develop your friendship with God remember what you pray about will depend on what is happening in your life. As in all good relationships we need to be flexible and constantly asking God to teach us how to pray and upgrade our communication with Him. When responsibilities in our life change, we should expect these to impact our prayer life too. Too often we try to maintain an old prayer pattern in a new season of life. While at university you may be able to develop a prayer rhythm with regular all nights of prayer but once you start commuting to work in London, and are on the train at 6am every day, these patterns need to shift for your sanity! Often we can feel condemned that we are losing our passion for prayer if our talking time with God gets shorter but the truth is, we are adjusting to a different season of life. Ask God to show you the appropriate times and rhythms of prayer that He wants from you in this season of your life. Remember He is your friend and loves to have time with you – this is not a duty!

Jesus was able to recognize his times and seasons, and was comfortable to refuse wrong demands from people. In John 7:6 we read:

"Therefore Jesus told them, 'My time is not yet here; for you any time will do'."

Jesus grew up in Nazareth, worked as a carpenter, but only started to minister at thirty years old. He was very aware of His times and seasons and used the phrase, *"My time has not yet come"* on several occasions in His life when he was being pressured by others to do more. We need to recognize that there is a time for family and children and this is not just waiting time or wasted time but an investment for you and your next generation. Often this will affect your available time for prayer but ask God to show you how to pray in the busy season of small children. There are times to care for elderly parents, times to invest in further training and education, and many other seasons of life. All these seasons will have different demands upon your time and your available time for God but be ready to change and make time to talk in the new season. We need to make the decision that we cannot afford NOT to pray and so become determined to find a place and space to have great times talking to God.

As we finish this chapter, let us pray together that God will give you wisdom as you build a life of prayer.

Prayer:

Father, today I ask you again – Teach me how to pray! I want to learn how to communicate with you in my own personal and individual language and style. Father, I am asking you to stretch my fluency and my experience of prayer. Teach me to enjoy spending time with you and let me experience a vibrant atmosphere of love and passion for you as I pray. Give me a fresh understanding of the mandate and areas of responsibility you are asking me to pray for. Let me know my times and seasons so that I may give myself willingly to times of prayer when you call me to spend time with you. Thank you for a fresh impartation of grace to pray! Amen.

Talking Time with God

DEVELOPING A DEVOTIONAL PRAYER LIFE

BACK TO BASICS – SIMPLE PRAYER WORKS

As we decide to give ourselves to the place of prayer we need to realize prayer is not complicated. Most of us have had a crisis and just cried out, "Oh God, help!", and received an instantaneous miraculous answer. Those simple cries of the heart touch God. Sometimes, with all our training, knowledge and information we can lose our simplicity. Effective prayer does not have to be complicated. Essentially, good prayer is about you being relaxed with God, remembering that He is your friend, not your critic. Simple prayer does work.

Too often we focus on ourselves and our inabilities rather than on God and His abilities. "I don't think I can pray for that because I'm not big enough...I don't have enough faith...I can't find the right words." But prayer is all about connecting to how big God is and does not depend on how great or small we are. When my husband, Gordon, and I were working with Reinhard Bonnke we had an associate evangelist working with us, Kenneth Meshoe, who had an amazing healing ministry. Kenneth's daughter, who was about four years old at the time, would walk behind him as he prayed for literally hundreds of people at a time. Everyone's eyes were always on the "big evangelist", but following behind him praying for every person would be his little girl who could only reach people's knees! Kenneth would pray for each person and move on and then came his daughter copying her dad. Often after this little girl had finished praying and moved on with her dad, the person would exclaim, "I can see" or "I can hear". Onlookers would have probably attributed these healings to Kenneth's ministry, but I often wondered to myself, was it the prayers of this little girl that God had answered? Simple prayers work!

When we are faced with a big problem we think we need to find a "big" prayer. No! Just let the cries for help come naturally and God will hear and answer. We need to be sensitive to the Spirit and let Him direct our prayer. There will be times when you will not pray according to your style of personal preference but just let the God-sound of your heart be released. Remember: simple, sincere, honest prayer is what is important to God in this prayer relationship that you are building. God once said to me, "Simple prayers from your hungry heart will always touch mine – so speak. I am listening!"

KEEP IT SIMPLE

I grew up in India as a little girl. My father was a minister in Bombay Baptist Church and we lived above the church. On one particular Sunday, I was around four and a half years old at the time, my father was downstairs conducting the evening meeting and a lady from the church was putting me to bed. As she was doing so, I turned to her and said, "Please can I have Jesus in my heart?" Reportedly, this was my prayer: I took hold of my pillow, hugged it very tight and said, "Dear Lord Jesus, I want you to be as close to me for the rest of my life, as my pillow is right now." It worked and I have loved Jesus ever since!

So you do not have to pray long, complicated prayers for them to have a lasting effect. Even when your prayers do not sound "super-spiritual" they can still have great spiritual power to bring change! I believe God loves answering our simple heart-felt prayer for everyday needs. Good prayer can be very practical. In Britain you quickly learn to start praying for parking places, as there never seem to be enough. I remember when my kids were tiny and still in their car seats, they would eagerly compete for the right to pray, "No, it's my turn to pray for the parking space!" God seemed to love their child-like passion and provided parking spaces for us again and again!

Good prayer has more to do with your heart attitude than with your verbal language. Do not pray corrective prayers that sound like you have your life in order and you are now asking God to please sort out the issues in another person. Remember, even if your life is blessed and secure, this is only because of the goodness of God to you. Remember that if God did not bless you and your marriage, your children, and your life, you too would be facing many difficulties. So do not pray from an exalted position that sounds like this: "Thank you God that our marriage is good and our kids are not on drugs and our daughter is not pregnant..." but pray with a heartfelt compassion that understands the pain of others' lives and serve them with kindness as you pray. Keep it simple and do not let any bitter judgement contaminate your prayers.

SPECIFIC PRAYER WORKS

If you aim at nothing, then you will usually hit it! Too often we do not know if our prayers are being answered because they are too vague and directionless. People often say that they have been praying for years, but do you know what you have been praying for? We can tend to pray "blanket" prayers for God's blessing. But what is the specific area you are asking God to bless? Unless you are specific with your requests to God, how do you know when they have been answered? We all need the encouragement of answered prayer to give us fresh impetus in our prayer lives, so be specific so that you can identify and quantify the results of your prayers.

Several years ago I visited a church in America that each year set a specific church prayer goal as a congregation. The previous year they felt God challenge them to believe for a financial breakthrough to repay the mortgage on their church property. As a church they began praying and as God blessed their personal finances they gave towards this project. By the end of that year the church mortgage payments had been completely reimbursed. Curious, I asked them, "What is your goal for this year?" They replied that God had spoken to them, that because they had honoured Him by settling the debt on His house, He now wanted them to target their personal debts and see what He would do. So the leaders asked the congregation to confidentially bring any information on a personal debt in sealed envelopes. They then placed this assortment of envelopes in a large basket at the front of the church and began to lay hands on this basket of needs each Sunday at a specific moment during their worship service. At first the basket was overflowing with many documents, but as each debt was completely paid, the relevant papers were removed from the basket, and the people literally watched the debt level of the church decrease as God did many financial miracles!

This is what we need to do. When we have a prayer need, whether great or small, we need to identify it, write it down and then specifically pray for it. So make sure that your prayer life has specific goals, so you can look and say, "Yes, I can see God answering my prayers." Some areas of your life are more difficult to quantify into specific requests, but make sure that somewhere in your prayer life you do have definite goals.

Children are very good at asking for specific requests. My son, David, really wanted to go skiing, so he began praying that he would be able to go. Before long we received an invitation to minister in Norway over the New Year period. The conference was to be held at a hotel. When David heard of this invitation he immediately asked, "Do they have skiing there?" Further investigation revealed that this particular hotel backed onto one of the best ski resorts in Norway! David said, "That's it! You don't need to pray about this invitation. This is God!" Bless him! He had been calling in the skiing holiday that he desperately wanted, and here it was! Maybe you think this is rather an audacious way to pray? But God didn't seem to mind and He answered David's prayer.

I find that children are good at challenging our concepts of our friendship with God. Our son, David, was born in Kenya but was only four years old when we left and moved back to England. However, as a teenager he developed an intense desire to go and see this land of his birthplace. We knew that this was becoming important to him, but at the time we did not have the funds to finance such a trip. David was disappointed but immediately responded that he was going to pray about it and ask God to pay his bill for him instead! Three days after this conversation, my parents came to visit from the USA and my Mum asked to speak to me privately. She took me to one side and asked, "We are going to Kenya in April and we just felt that maybe we should take David with us. What do you think?" I was so touched that God had heard David's cry and provided for him and so said, "Well, David has just started praying about this very issue. Do you want to speak to him?" We called David down from his room and asked him to chat with his grandparents. Moments later he emerged from the lounge ecstatic, "WOW, that's amazing. I didn't even have to wait for years and try to save up the money. God has just answered me!" My children have taught me so much about being unashamed with my specific prayer requests.

We should not only pray for our personal needs, but also stretch out the horizon of our prayers to encompass the needs of others and even whole communities. Those of us involved in praying for London soon learnt to focus our prayers for this great city – we were not simply praying, "God bless London." We began knocking on the doors of members of parliament, local councillors and educators, asking, "Will you tell us exactly what your needs are? We want to pray strategically and specifically. We want to know that we are praying where the community is hurting." As we did this, we saw some wonderful answers to our prayers.

A group of pastors in the London borough of Haringey decided to find out what the prayer needs of their community were and engage in focussed prayer in order to see some quantifiable results. They have seen many answers to prayer across the borough. Their community had many schools that were failing. In the UK, schools that are under-performing tend to have their government subsidies cut and so their annual budgets can become smaller and more difficult as a result. It is often disheartening as the already failing school becomes further under-resourced and fails even more. When the pastors visited the school authorities they were asked to pray for a significant improvement in the schools' performance and a corresponding increase in funding. So they prayed specifically over the next nine months that there would be a turnaround. Schools in England are rated in a national performance table and, during this year, the schools' rating moved from minus eight to plus seven! As a result, Haringey council sat up and noticed what these pastors were doing! Now the council emails the pastors with specific prayer requests on a regular basis!

STUBBORN PRAYER

Unfortunately most of us tend to be stubborn about the wrong things rather than for the right reason! All of us have the ability to dig our heels in and say, "No, I don't want to." If only we would apply the same kind of stubbornness to our prayer lives, so that once we began praying for something we did not give up easily. God wants us to have this kind of tenacity, a godly stubbornness when we pray. It is what the Bible calls *persistent prayer*. Many times in our prayer lives we struggle with being persistent, yet, endurance is an essential prayer quality. So let God awaken your stubbornness for breakthrough. Remember, now is not a good time to give up!

We all want to reap the harvest of our prayers, don't we? We patiently sow seeds of prayer and expect that in due course, they will bear fruit and we will reap a harvest. I believe God is saying prophetically that the harvest time is coming for *stubborn* prayers – those long-term prayers where you have prayed and prayed and nothing has seemed to happen. Maybe, instead of receiving the breakthrough, your situation became more impossible until you thought, "God, what are you doing here?" If that is true for you, then God wants to make a declaration to you now: *praying time is never wasted time.* There is going to be a harvest from your prayers. Every place where you have sown your prayers, especially with tears, the harvest is going to come.

MATURING IN OUR PRAYER LIVES

I believe, in these days, God is calling the Church to a new place of responsibility and maturity in prayer. We have heard the cry of the Holy Spirit saying, "Come on Church, it's time to grow up; time to take responsibility; time to take hold of your promises." We have wanted to stay as little children, and although in one sense we are always children of God, we should not remain as spiritual toddlers, never accepting our responsibility and the destiny call upon our lives.

As we grow up and take responsibility for the mandate on our life it does not mean we have to lose the intimacy and relationship with our Father. My daughter, Nicola, is the married mother of three children and leading a significant church with her husband, Tim. Although she is a mature woman with huge responsibilities she is still her daddy's little girl and Gordon and Nicola have a wonderful relationship. She has left home and now carries new responsibilities in her life; but she is still our child. In the same way, we are always children of the

Kingdom but we have got to get busy about our Father's business. Our Father has given us a commission and a job to do and *now* is the time to carry the good news of the Kingdom to our communities.

CONSISTENT PRAYER MIXED WITH FAITH

So in these days God is calling us to be an army of mature prayers who are consistent and persistent. Sometimes prayer does feel like hard work – it is just a committed routine of diligent hard work for the Kingdom. We don't only pray when we feel goose bumps; we don't pray because we feel anointed; we pray because we have been commanded to pray. We just do it! God is looking for that resolute consistency in His army – that we will pray without ceasing; we hold fast and we don't give up.

We need to be continually seeking our Father's face, saying, "God, we've got nowhere else to go! We are committed to stay with you!" All of us can remember a time in our life when we simply obeyed our parents' wishes, even though we wanted to do something totally different. We did not obey our parents because *we felt like it*; we just obeyed because of *our respect for their authority*. There are times when it is the same in the Kingdom of God – you just need to obey even when it feels tough. Obedience has power. So decide to pray because God has asked you to do this regardless of whether it feels "anointed" or not. We need to press in and have an attitude that says, "God, I am not going anywhere. I am committed to walk this faith journey with you. I may not like everything about this season right now but I have come too far to give up and I will reap from this prayer investment."

GOD GIVES GOOD BONUSES

Hebrews 6:10 promises us:

> "God is not unjust; he will not forget your work and the love you have shown him as you have helped his people and continue to help them."

God loves to reward those who work for Him. Often we do not consider prayer as one of these services with a reward. So I would like us to reflect on this verse in relation to our prayer life. When we pray for others we are "serving" them. God is not unjust. He doesn't forget that service. The writer of Hebrews continues:

> "We want each of you to show this same diligence to the very end, in order to make your hope sure. We do not want you to become lazy, but to imitate those who through faith and patience inherit what has been promised." (Hebrews 6:11-12)

When praying for something, we can often start off with a great sense of enthusiasm, which then peters out, but we need to finish our prayer journey with the same sense of expectancy as when we started out. Faith and patience working together win the day and we get to receive our bonus – our reward. Too often we get lazy and stop praying too soon but it is time for that consistent prayer, mixed with faith, to win through.

God spoke to me one morning, "Rachel, usually unanswered prayer is not a wrong prayer, just an unfinished one." Sometimes when we pray into a situation and nothing happens immediately, we give up. We think that, because we cannot see any visible change in the circumstances yet, our prayer must be worthless. But it is much more likely that we simply haven't prayed for long enough, and we need to push through all the way to the end.

MIND THE GAP PLEASE!

Anyone who has travelled on the London underground trains in recent years will be familiar with the voice over the loud speaker system constantly reminding the people to, "Mind the gap, please – Mind the gap!", as the doors open and people get on and off the crowded underground trains. In the same way God is calling to His prayer army to stand and "mind the gap" between people's lives and promises. Look at any situation and you will be able to identify this gap between what God wants for the community and the reality of what they are experiencing. Heaven is declaring, "Let His Kingdom come", but earth is out of alignment. With one hand we are laying hold of heaven's desire and, with the other, earth's reality, and we need to draw these two realms together by prayer. We pray, "Lord, let your Kingdom come now to *this* place at *this* time." You touch the throne of God; you take God's prophetic word which He has spoken over that place and then close this gap with the arms of faith. Everything around you can shout, "Don't bother, give up, you're a failure!" But you need to become stubborn and refuse to give up your position of faith. Hold fast and watch for the joy of breakthrough.

NOW IS NOT A GOOD TIME TO GIVE UP!

Galatians 6:9 says:

> *"Let us not become weary in doing good, for at the proper time we will reap a harvest if we do not give up."*

Your prayer life is probably far more effective than you could ever realize so don't stop now. It is so easy to become tired and just give up. The enemy would love you to believe that the delay to the answers to your prayers is because you are a bad person, or that you do not know how to pray the "real" powerful ones that work. In actual fact, you are praying the right prayers, but you just need to keep praying them – you are doing well – so don't get weary.

One of the most common pitfalls in prayer is *weariness*. Most of us, if we look back at situations we prayed for, will say, "Yes, I got really tired in that season and gave up praying." That's why it is so important to have prayer partners to encourage us. We need people to cheer us on. We need people to say, "Hey! You are doing well!" If we seek to help one another in prayer, to minister encouragement, then it will be much easier to complete that course.

Prayer will develop your spiritual muscles: you will get tired as it takes practice and effort. As we pray we are establishing this statement: "Thy kingdom COME on earth as it is in Heaven!" Prayer is about bringing this alignment between the spiritual and natural destiny. Things that are decreed in Heaven need to be established on the earth through prayer. When that process is complete, the physical answer to our prayer is revealed. In the book of Ephesians we are instructed to wrestle in prayer but not against flesh and blood, rather against the spiritual powers. What we need to note is this: we are called to wrestle but just be careful about what and with whom you are wrestling! As we begin to pray, we start this process of alignment between the spiritual and the natural, so that, eventually, at the "proper" time, we will receive the harvest of our prayers. This is what the apostle Paul calls "the fullness of time" or the "proper" time. It is a God-ordained *kairos* moment when Heaven and earth touch and we see the breakthrough we need. So keep wrestling and develop those muscles!

SATISFACTION

Psalm 30 verse 5 says: "*Weeping may endure for a night, but joy comes in the morning!*" There are times when our prayer life needs to be tenacious and press through, but get ready for the breakout of joy! I love the stories of answered prayer. Standing in front of me was a father in tears: "I never thought this was going to happen. This is amazing!", he exclaimed. Slowly, through his tears, the father told me that his fifteen year old son who had reacted against anything Christian had just walked forward in the summer camp meeting and given his life to God. His son was now on his knees, crying, as God touched his life. "At last God has answered my prayers, I cannot believe it, I am SO happy", the father cried. The Church needs to remember that this place of prayer is a place of incredible joy.

Isaiah 56:7 says:

> *"These I will bring to my holy mountain and give them joy in my house of prayer."*

As you begin to spend more time in prayer, God is going to take you on a journey. He wants to take you up onto the mountaintops into new places of intimacy and He wants to give you outrageous fun and joy in His house of prayer. Isaiah continues:

> *"These burnt offerings and sacrifices will be accepted on my altar."* *(Isaiah 56:7)*

It costs us something to pray; but God will reward your times of trial with great joy! Praying is such a privilege. Expect a new season of enjoyment. God is going to give you joy in the house of prayer.

 # Healthy Rhythms of Prayer

BUILDING A CREATIVE HOUSE OF PRAYER

A HOUSE OF PRAYER FOR YOU

Now let us explore the different expressions and creative ways that we can pray. Too often we can get stuck in a repetitive routine and lose our sense of creativity so I hope these ideas will help you to break out into new areas of expression in your prayer life. At the end of the previous chapter we read in Isaiah 56:7 that God wants to give us "joy in the house of prayer." So, for a moment, I want you to imagine that you are building and designing a house to be your personal home. Whenever people build a house for themselves they take time to incorporate their personal preferences and colours into the building. They restore, renovate and paint it to suit their likes and needs. Similarly, as we begin to build our personal *house of prayer* we need to build a place that feels like home to us.

Too often, when we are establishing our own personal prayer life, we just adopt other people's methods, assuming they will work for us, when really we should be exploring our own style. In these days I believe God is restoring a new freedom of individual expression into the place of prayer just as He has done in our times of worship. In the past, much of our worship was very structured, but now the Holy

Spirit has breathed life into our worship and we express ourselves more freely with new sounds and songs. In the same way God wants to expand the creativity in our corporate prayer times and take us out of the contained box in which we have lived for so long.

God once said to me regarding prayer, "It's time to colour outside your lines." I had a very regimented idea about the do's and don'ts of prayer. My prayer life was very rules orientated and as a result I often felt a failure. However, God is a God of principles rather than strict rules: we need to understand that living by Godly principles is different from obeying a list of strict rules. A rule says, if you step over this line you will be punished, irrespective of the reason. But a principle is able to weigh the pros and cons of the situation. For example, in principle I made sure my children were in bed before 8.00pm most nights when they were under ten years old, but if my family came to visit or it was a special occasion we coloured outside the lines and the children went to bed late! As you read this chapter, remember that I am sharing principles with you, not rules. I trust that these principles will help you to build the basic structure for your life of prayer. But the final décor of this house of prayer is yours; everyone's house will be different, because this is *your* building adventure. You are the architect of your house of prayer and you are creating a meeting place for God. Isn't that fantastic? You are building something that has your personal touch of creative expression into which you will welcome Jesus.

LIVING A LIFESTYLE OF PRAYER

Prayer needs to become your lifestyle, not just a meeting you attend on a Wednesday evening for one hour. All of us need to develop an attitude that we are ready to communicate with God at any time, and that we expect Him to be involved with every area of our lives. God wants us to have a constant awareness of Him, talking about everyday needs and even the most mundane of things. But He also desires dedicated times of intimacy with Him alone. Prayer on the run is fine, as long as we make time for God alone too. A healthy prayer life is like a healthy marriage: it is necessary to talk about the everyday issues but there also needs to be those special times where you are alone, just the two of you, with no interruptions, to talk more deeply. In your prayer life there needs to be this balance too. You need times when you can pour out your heart to God and wait long enough to hear His answer. These times of stillness are precious when it is just you and God, sitting with one another, face to face, heart to heart, and you talk and listen. I call these intimacy moments – "table for two" time!

Good communication in a healthy relationship needs to have a mixture of general administrative communication with more personal and intimate time. This works both in a marriage and with prayer. In these moments you are saying to God, "This is a time that I have set aside just for you. There's nobody else, just you and me. No other pressures will intrude on our time together." This creates a real opportunity for talking heart to heart in the secret place.

TAKING "TABLE FOR TWO" TIME

Most of us discover that there is never a convenient time to pray. When was the last time you set time aside just to be alone and speak with God? When did you last spend time talking to God without a crisis or a pressing need motivating you? God is calling His bride, "Come away with me, let us spend time together" – and we need to respond. I believe this is why so many retreat and prayer centres have opened in recent years. They provide us with a place where we can go and meet with God away from the many distractions and demands.

All of us need to get away and spend time alone with God, but this is especially true for leaders. It takes a significant adjustment in the mind of a leader to come to God's Word just for himself. All leaders need times when they can take off their ministry "hat" and just come as themselves before God, not because of their responsibilities in the church, but as a child. Developing this discipline can take time and often needs a shifting of our mind-sets. If you are a leader, then plan to take about three days away each year just to sit in God's presence, to renew your perspective and receive from Him for yourself.

POSITIONS FOR PRAYER

Once you have decided to have some "table for two" time with God, how do you pray? What tools can help you to build your house of prayer? In the latter section of this chapter I want to discuss several distinct types of prayer, but before that let us look at the different positions we can choose when we pray. Each position will change the atmosphere in which you pray. When you bow before God it sets a different ambiance than when you stand to pray. So ask God to teach you to position yourself for prayer.

STAND UP

The position of your body is a powerful means of communication. We are taught this in business or in the classroom. If you walk into a room and the people stand up, it says something. Often people will stand because they want to create an atmosphere of honour and respect. Remaining seated can be a non-threatening sign meaning, "You are welcome here", or it can mean "I do not consider you my equal so I will sit in your presence!" Standing in God's presence to pray declares something, it releases a sense of honour towards God – we are saying, "I stand in awe of you".

Standing can also be a stance of faith. In Ephesians chapter 6 we read in verse 11 that we should "*Put on the whole armour of God, so that you may be able to stand against the schemes of the devil*". In times of battle I often find that I stand to pray as I declare that God is with us.

SIT DOWN

There is a place for the standing warrior prayer, but there is also the seated prayer of authority. In Ephesians 1:20-22 (NIV) we read:

> "...when he raised Christ from the dead and seated him at his right hand in the heavenly realms, far above all rule and authority, power and dominion, and every name that is invoked, not only in the present age but also in the one to come. And God placed all things under his feet and appointed him to be head over everything for the church."

Here we read that Christ is seated in heavenly places with authority over all spiritual powers and rulers. Then in Ephesians 2:4 we read that we have also been raised to be seated with Christ in these heavenly places. So here, in these scriptures, we are challenged to be seated with Christ far above all the powers and rulers. This is a position of authority and rulership over all the enemy's plans and power. Again in Psalm 23 we read about being seated at a table in the midst of our enemies. This is a position of security and authority in the midst of a time of contest.

However, being seated can also be the position of intimacy. We read that Mary sat at the feet of Jesus and listened to Him. This is a time when we are positioned to be more receptive, waiting upon God and listening to hear what He will say to us. Just this change of position can alter the way in which you pray and your expectation as you pray.

ON MY KNEES – AGAIN!

I love this position of prayer. When I know I need to pray but feel too overwhelmed and distracted there is something powerful about stopping, kneeling into the sofa or bed, putting your head into soft cushions or a mattress, taking a moment to focus and then just praying out loud. This kneeling prayer position immediately puts things into perspective. We come and hide in a Big God and realize we are just "little me"! We need to remind ourselves of the awesome power of our amazing God but remember He is our Father and he is ready to act on our behalf. Kneeling is a good way of reminding ourselves that we are dependent on Him and acknowledging His care. "I kneel before you Almighty God and know that you care for me. I hide myself in the shelter of your steadfast love and know you hear my cry." If you are feeling anxious or overwhelmed then kneel before your Father and let Him take care of you and your circumstances. Psalm 95:6 says:

> "Oh come, let us worship and bow down; let us **kneel** before the Lord, our Maker!"

BE PROSTRATE – FACE FIRST

Sometimes we need to just stop – rest and simply lie down in God's presence. To lie down before God in a public or even private place can make you feel very exposed and requires trust. But when you are weary and have been holding your world together in your own strength there comes a time when we need to let go and let God get close. We need to come and lie in His presence and say, "You are my God, please take all my burdens, fears and exhaustion". This is how we cast all our cares upon the Lord. There is something very wonderful about just lying in the Father's presence like this and letting His kindness minister to you. In Psalm 23 we read:

> "The LORD is my shepherd; I shall not want. He makes me lie down in green pastures. He leads me beside still waters. He restores my soul". (Psalm 23:1-3)

I wonder if you have ever thought about this phrase, *He **makes me** lie down in green pastures.* I believe there are times in our life where God needs us to stop and lie down. So take a moment and ask God to teach you the secret of resting in His presence, where you can lie down and acknowledge His power and strength and be open and vulnerable to Him.

RIGHT PLACE – RIGHT SPACE

As you develop your style and rhythm of prayer, think about the settings in which you choose to pray. Often we establish a set routine and every day we sit in the same place with the same view and pray through the same list of requests. But the place where you pray can also influence how you express yourself. I am sure you agree that you will pray very differently if you are sitting alone on the side of a high mountain with a clear view, compared to sitting in the coffee shop of a busy market square. Praying by water can often be a wonderful inspiration for times of prayer; walking or sitting by a stream can stimulate a different language of your heart. What about praying by the sea as you stand watching the awesome power of the waves? Maybe you do not live near to the coast or any kind of water, but sometimes it is worth travelling to somewhere special just to pray. When you are on vacation, enjoy the different scenery and let it stir you to pray. Take a moment to think about what scenery would evoke a different kind of prayer in you. Different atmospheres will stir different kinds of communication and expression.

Prayer drives – in the car again

Most of us spend many hours in the car each week. So can you drive and use this time to pray effectively? Yes, I have found that you can, but please keep your eyes open! There was a season in my life when I was doing a long drive to work by myself and God challenged me to use this time to learn to pray in the Spirit. So I would look at the clock and say to myself, "OK, now I'm going to pray in my prayer language and build up my spirit-man for five minutes." Then I would just pray in my heavenly prayer language. At first I was amazed how hard I found it to pray without stopping even for five minutes. I thought it would be easy, but it wasn't. So I made it into a kind of spiritual weight-lifting exercise: let's see if I can do five minutes of spiritual "press ups" and then stretch it a bit further next time. In time I found I had a new fluency and found it easy to pray from my spirit. So, next time you are driving, why not ask the Lord, "How can I use this time – how should I pray?"

Walk and talk

Personally, walking and talking with God is my favourite thing. But I do have the best chocolate Labrador prayer partner that follows me on every trip. Fortunately it is difficult to walk and sleep so I find this an easy way to pray in the early mornings. The dog is always happy when he sees me reaching for my particular walking shoes as he knows we will walk over the fields and it gives me space with Jesus before the rush of a busy day. If you want to pray for your neighbours or your city, there is no better way than to get out and walk the streets. People tend to pray differently outside buildings than inside them, so prayer walking brings a fresh dimension to your prayer life. Maybe you already do this individually, but what about groups of people or the whole church going prayer walking? We tend to have the mentality that corporate prayer only takes place inside a building. So why don't you take your church outside and have a prayer meeting?

In the bath or shower

This might raise a smile, but I had a good friend who was powerfully touched by God in her bath! Angela really wanted God to give her a new prayer language and to be able to speak in tongues, but for some reason she could never get through. So I said to her, "Where do you relax the most?" and she replied, "In the bath, I suppose." So I gave her this advice: "Next time you are in the house on your own, fill your bath up, put in lots of bubble bath, relax, and just begin to thank God and ask Him to fill you with His Spirit." So she planned a time, got in the bath, prayed, and God filled her with His Spirit and she spoke in her prayer language for the first time. The next time I saw her she was so excited. She rushed up to me and said, "Rachel, it worked! At last I was relaxed. God connected with me and I had the breakthrough." I know many people who have some of their best worship times in the shower. God is ready to connect with us anytime we are ready to talk.

Even when sleeping?

Can you pray when you are asleep – I thought we should stay awake!? I believe that, even when our physical body is asleep, our spirit can be wide awake. So as I go to sleep each night I say, "Lord, even as I am asleep, speak to my spirit." As a result, many of the revelatory thoughts for my sermons have been received as I sleep! God tends to give me headlines or phrases that I remember when I awake and they trigger my thinking and I know that the Holy Spirit has dictated these ideas to me in my sleep. In Psalm 16 we read this scripture:

> "I will praise the LORD, who counsels me; **even at night my heart instructs me**." (Psalm 16:7)

So, why not experiment with these different positions and places for prayer and see if you pray differently? Ask God to give you wisdom to build a creative house of prayer for your life.

DIFFERENT TYPES AND EXPRESSIONS OF PRAYER

We have looked at the positions and places which can influence the way we pray. But now I want to look more closely at the different expressions and types of prayer that can become part of our prayer language. In reality there are hundreds of different ways in which we can express what is in our heart, but let's look at some of these examples in more detail.

SUPPLICATION – CRY GRACE

Supplication is a prayer that cries out for grace. It has a strong sense of appeal. One Bible commentator has illustrated it in terms of a dog begging for a biscuit from his master. Imagine you are eating a chocolate biscuit and there is a dog sitting in front of you. The way in which that dog's eyes look at you longingly – that's supplication!

Supplication is a heart that is crying out to God just as Habakkuk did:

> "Oh God in wrath, remember mercy." (Habakkuk 3:2)

Supplication is a prayer from the knees that pleads, "God we are your people. Please do not give us what we deserve, but hear our cry in these days and answer us. Hear our cry for mercy. We need your help – Oh God come!" Supplicative prayer is a raw cry that does not sound very elegant. It is an emotional prayer, with the sound of a strong, heartfelt appeal. As you read the Psalms you will find this prayer again and again as David calls out to God to help him, deliver him, rescue him and save him!

ASK – PLEASE CAN I HAVE...!

Sometimes all we need to do when we pray is simply come and ask. In Matthew 7:7 we read the simple command, "Ask and it will be given to you." Here this Greek verb is constructed in its present-continuous-active form, so in English it carries the sense of, "Ask and keep on asking and it will be given and keep on being given to you." This kind of prayer requires us to live with an everyday, childlike dependency on God. We need to live with an asking attitude that willingly asks our Father for help. Because of our fear of being too demanding, or our fierce independence, we usually feel we cannot ask for all our mundane needs of life as this would be asking too much of God: "Who are we to keep bothering God with all our requests? Isn't it a bit presumptuous or needy?" But we must remember that we are the children of God and, as our Father, He delights to provide for us. If you have children then you know that they are not shy about asking for anything! Our needs are not a nuisance to God: He wants to hear our voice. Asking should be part of our natural relationship with our Father in Heaven.

Neither does God limit the size of our ask. In fact he encourages us to think BIG. The prayer of petition should include your everyday personal needs, but in Psalm 2:8 God challenges us to ask on a larger scale too. *"Ask of me and I will give you the nations as your inheritance. The ends of the earth for your possession."* What an amazing privilege to be encouraged to ask God for a nation. Often people find the idea of "asking" for a nation a little overwhelming but it is not complicated; just ask and keep it simple and specific. Then as you begin to simply ask, God will give you a connection with that nation in your heart and He will begin to speak to you, revealing things that you can pray for. Soon you discover that what began as a simple asking prayer, has developed into a deeper prayer conversation and very soon it has become intercession for the people and land.

THANK YOU – THE PRAYER OF THANKSGIVING

Often we can be lazy when it comes to saying thank you, especially to God. I found the Holy Spirit had to teach me this true attitude of gratitude. I used to think I was a grateful person, but God has shown me just how much I take for granted and how unthankful I can be. We can develop an attitude of entitlement, just expecting God to sort out our issues because that is His job, which kills any sense of thankfulness. Have you ever prayed with someone about an issue and later discovered via a third party that the prayer had been answered, but the person concerned never told you? You might even go and ask them, "Why didn't you tell me?" Usually the reply will be, "I forgot!" How can we forget to say thank you when someone is healed, or a baby is miraculously conceived, or a financial situation suddenly turned around? But unfortunately we have all done it.

We need to ask God to cultivate a fresh attitude of gratitude in our lives. Often, when Paul summarises his final instructions to the believers in his epistles, you will find on his list "thanksgiving".

We can see an example of this in Philippians 4:5-6:

> "Rejoice in the Lord always, and again I say it rejoice. Let your gentleness be evident to all for the Lord is near. Do not be anxious about anything, but in **everything by prayer and petition with thanksgiving**, present your request to God."

What a perfect mix: thanksgiving blended with the prayer of asking.

In Psalm 100:4 it says:

> "I will enter His gates with thanksgiving in my heart."

We are much more likely to listen to a person who comes to us with a thankful attitude than one who complains. This atmosphere of thanksgiving is so appealing to the heart of God. One day God showed me how often I forget this key in my relationship with Him. On this particular day I had managed to achieve all I wanted to do before the kids came home from school and I was eagerly waiting for them to arrive. Then, sure enough, I heard the back gate go, footsteps along the passage and then the back door open. But the first words I heard were, "Mum, why is my football kit dirty?" and all my excitement evaporated. I had looked forward to everyone arriving back home, hoping that they would enjoy the treats I had cooked and be grateful. But as I heard this angry demand the Holy Spirit spoke to me: "Rachel, I wait in eager expectation for your footsteps. I anticipate your time with me and wait for your voice too. But so often when you open the door of your heart I hear the accusation demanding, 'God what is happening?' You enter my presence with an attitude of anger or complaint rather than gratitude." Needless to say, this challenged me. We need to practise entering God's presence with thanksgiving!

I CONFESS – I WAS WRONG!

Most of us are not very good at saying "I am sorry". But this prayer of confession needs to be a vital aspect of our Christian life. We would all lead much happier lives, free from shame and guilt, if we learnt to come and say, "Dear Jesus, please forgive me, I am sorry. I have messed up." All of us regularly make poor choices and we need to confess our failure before we can move on with our life, cleansed and free. We need to regularly come before the cross and say, "I'm sorry, Lord, I have made a poor choice. I have sinned." If we deal with our sin honestly, we also deal with the shame and our sense of failure. Too many people walk around troubled by condemnation, feeling like second-class Christians. But if you confess your sin and repent, you can enter the place of intimacy with God and enjoy His presence without feeling guilty. You stand righteous, clean and redeemed because you have handed the failure to Jesus.

We need to realize that the prayer of confession is not a prayer of failure but rather a prayer of release. 1 John 1:9 says:

> "If we confess our sins, he is faithful and just and will forgive our sins and purify us from all unrighteousness."

Notice that this verse says "if". So if we want to live with the reward, we need to take action. My husband, Gordon, always says, "God forgives the guilty but not the pathetic." He explains that so often we come into God's presence with our pathetic excuses, justifying why we have sinned, blaming circumstances or other people, but if we will take responsibility for our decisions and confess our mistakes, then God will purify us. So, as part of building your house of prayer, you should build a confessional room and visit it regularly to say you are sorry.

I FORGIVE YOU – PLEASE WALK FREE!

Most parents find it is difficult to train their children to say: "I'm sorry" and "I forgive you" and mean it! The sad thing is, we are not much more mature in the Church. We find it difficult to apologise and take responsibility for our wrong attitudes and even more challenging to forgive and release people from their poor behaviour towards us. But I believe that these two prayers of confession and forgiveness, prayed from the heart, are a powerful combination.

We need to consider the power of the prayer of forgiveness both on a personal and a corporate level. When was the last time you attended a church service based on the theme of forgiveness? I believe that, if we as churches regularly prayed together along this theme of forgiveness, so much of the pain and offence that people carry could be healed. Unfortunately, people often leave their churches when they get offended with someone. When this happens the issue is rarely dealt with and so division and conflict wounds the Church once again. But if we could learn how to forgive one another, it could save us so much heartbreak in our relationships.

The prayer of forgiveness requires you to have an attitude of generosity; it will cost you something to forgive a person who has offended you. Rarely do the people who mistreat you come to you, realize their mistake, and apologize first. Usually people are totally unaware of the extent of the pain that their actions have caused you, but nevertheless you must still forgive them. Just as Jesus cried out from the cross, "*Father, forgive them. They don't know what they are doing*", so we must learn to forgive others regardless of their attitude towards us. Often we are hurt by well-meaning people who honestly do not realize that they have offended us. They may never realize how their actions affected us, but we need to make a choice to forgive them regardless. Remember it is your life that will be affected by this choice to forgive or withhold – you need to regularly pray this prayer of generous forgiveness so that you can live your life completely free from all bitterness!

While considering this subject of forgiveness, please remember to forgive yourself too. Learning to navigate this journey of forgiveness can be challenging for most of us. Finally we come to a place where we are willing to relinquish our rights and forgive others but we can still carry a deep unforgiveness towards ourselves. While being generous towards other people's failures, we find ourselves unable to forget our own, and so live with crippling regret. Ask God to show you the power of His forgiveness to set your own heart free. If God has forgiven you then you need to forgive yourself and release the memory of your past failures.

SILENCE – THE PRAYER BEYOND WORDS
Good communication does not just depend on spoken words. Most of us will remember that parental look across the dining table when there were visitors present for dinner. In that one focussed stare, where not a word was spoken, you knew you were being warned and, if you continued to misbehave, you were going to be disciplined. The power of a silent look!

We should use our times of silence to practise our communication skills with God. Develop this simple technique by thinking of a particular attribute of God – His love, His majesty or His faithfulness – and then focus on that attribute, while silently giving thanks for that aspect of His character. As you do this, your thoughts will rise as simple prayers that touch God, even though no actual words are spoken. If you sit silently for a time before God, focussing on Him in this way, you will sense the sweetness of His presence. There are times to shout and declare the goodness of God in prayer but there are also times of silent intimacy, when words seem totally inappropriate, and all that is needed is the silent heart to heart communication. In these moments, the relationship between you and your God moves beyond words, and you find that your spirit is communicating as deep calls to deep.

In these silent times of prayer you can develop the art of listening so that God can reveal His strategies for your life. This rhythm of prayer allows God the opportunity to share His heart with you. Too often we enter our prayer times with our own agenda and, once we have presented our list of needs, we are ready to head for the door, not realizing that we are missing our chance to hear what the Holy Spirit wants to say to us in response. Whenever you pray, you should always allow time for God to speak back to you. So much of hearing God is nothing to do with dramatic voices booming down from the heavens; it is about learning to recognize God's gentle nudges, the instincts of the Spirit. God's voice can be as subtle as a thought but when it comes you know – this was not my idea but a God thought.

When Gordon and I were pastoring, we learnt to depend on the wisdom of these quiet words spoken into our hearts during times of waiting on Him. I remember one day, on our day off, I just kept thinking about one particular woman in our church. In the end I said, "Gordon, I really feel that we need to go and buy this lady some flowers and pop round and see her quickly before we go out for the day." So we did and, when we arrived, she said to us, "Oh, I wondered if you would remember me today." As she spoke I was frantically trying to remember what occasion we should be remembering. But the flowers seemed to be a perfect gesture as she continued, saying, "It was a year ago today that my husband died and I wondered if anyone in the church would remember." As she spoke I knew that I hadn't remembered but the Holy Spirit had. So I was able to say to this lady, "To tell you the truth, I didn't remember, but the Holy Spirit did and He told me I was to come and bring you these flowers today."

HEAVENLY CONVERSATIONS – PRAYING IN THE SPIRIT
Jude chapter 1 verse 20 encourages us:

> *"And build yourself up in your most holy faith. Pray in the Spirit."*

Praying in the Spirit is something people either love or hate. Unfortunately the whole area of "speaking in tongues", or praying in the Spirit, has become a divisive issue in some churches but I think we need to pray both with our understanding and in the Spirit. Prayer should be a supernatural conversation which is informed and inspirational.

You probably have several entrances to your house: a front door, a rear or side door, and maybe a patio door. However, most of us will tend to use the same door to go into our house whenever we return home. We can have a similar routine in our prayer lives too. We get into a habit of approaching our times of prayer by using the same style and language each time we pray. Often our prayer becomes boring because we get stuck in a dull repetitive routine. Well, try using a different "door" to enter your place of prayer! If you usually start your prayer time by praying in tongues, balance it with the good discipline of praying with your understanding too.

However, praying in the Spirit is good for your life and is like giving your "spiritual man" a regular vitamin tonic. In 1 Corinthians 14:4 it says that a person who speaks in the spirit edifies himself. If you examine the root of this word "to edify" it literally means "to grow, enlarge, increase, and give an increased capacity to". So if you feel like your spirit is under-nourished and you need some more spiritual muscle, then increase your praying time in the Spirit! The Holy Spirit will grow and increase your spiritual capacity and enlarge your ability and effectiveness to hear God for your life. You will find that praying in the Spirit regularly will strengthen your stamina and ability to pray and increase your wisdom and revelation.

MY LETTER TO GOD – A WRITTEN PRAYER

Some regard written prayers, like the Anglican liturgy, as belonging to an outdated, traditional style of worship which is no longer needed. But I believe there is incredible power in written prayer and I am sure, like me, you really appreciate reading the Psalms. These powerful prayers still touch many lives today. Written prayers can also be a helpful tool in corporate prayer times. They bring a sense of focus and purpose as the congregation repeat this specially crafted prayer together. If a leadership team takes time to pray and then write a prayer of declaration that the church can pray together, it can be a very powerful aid in unified prayer. Whenever God's people come together with one voice, one heart, one mind, focussed on a specific goal or vision, powerful results can be achieved.

But written crafted prayers are for more than our congregational services. Remember the "table for two" picture? There is something very intimate and beautiful when we take time to write a letter from our heart to God in prayer. In the Hickson household we have a tradition: on every birthday, each Christmas, or other special occasion, we expect Gordon to write a special poem to capture the moment. These poems are amazing and I love the way these written words carry such depth and intimacy, capturing each special family moment forever. So let me encourage you to take some time on your prayer journey of life and write a letter to God expressing your heart. Remember, written words have a special legacy.

COLOUR OUTSIDE THE LINES – CREATIVE ART AND PRAYER

So what about the use of paint or dance during our times of prayer? We need to recognize that our spiritual communication is not limited to words alone. All over the world we are witnessing a new release of artistic creativity in the church. For too long we have limited our definition of prayer to just our spoken communication, but the younger generation are much more visual and multimedia orientated when they pray. If you go into any teenager's bedroom, it's not uncommon to find them talking on the phone, with their music playing in the background, watching the TV, while attempting to do their school work on their computer, all at the same time! So time in the house of prayer will need to be much more interactive, especially if we want to engage our young people. We need to allow new levels of creativity to invade our traditional prayer spaces.

In the last years I have watched people paint pictures during times of worship and prayer and through their art they express powerful concepts which communicate something profound beyond words. I have also been deeply moved watching people dance their story of love and devotion towards God. I remember a service where a group of dancers portrayed the sacrifice of the cross and I found myself on my knees in gratitude and tears.

All these different languages of communication can evoke from us different expressions of prayer and devotion. Unfortunately I am not very gifted at expressing myself through paint, dance and poems but I still love the challenge of being stimulated by these more creative ways of communicating to God. These days our prayer meetings often include different prayer stations with focussed activities which help articulate our prayer through various activities in addition to words. Different people will have different triggers. Some of us are stimulated by what we see, by vibrant colours, so watching a painting take shape as described previously will trigger prayer for you while, for others, it is the sound of music. Ask God to show you how you can embrace some of these ideas and move beyond just words to enhance your communication in the place of prayer.

SING TO THE LORD – A NEW SONG
Musicians often say that they find it hard to pray fluently without music around them to stimulate their spirit. So if you are musical you need

to acknowledge that your spiritual language will be expressed more easily through notes, chords and sounds, rather than just spoken words. When you want to pray, pick up your guitar and start to strum, or sit at your keyboard and start to play, and you will soon find that your spirit is alive and you are praying. You may struggle to find your fluency when you are just sitting quietly and trying to talk but every time you sit at the keyboard and play, you immediately connect and start to communicate. I believe using your music is an essential part of a musician's prayer life. This is how you talk!

The Bible encourages us to come with songs when we enter the presence of God. In Colossians 3:16-17 we read:

> "Let the message of Christ dwell among you richly as you teach and admonish one another with all wisdom through psalms, hymns, and songs from the Spirit, singing to God with gratitude in your hearts. And whatever you do, whether in word or deed, do it all in the name of the Lord Jesus, giving thanks to God the Father through him."

These songs do not need to be expertly composed but can be a spontaneous song from the heart. We need to boldly break the sound barrier, even if our voice is not the best, and let God hear our new songs of joy. Even if you are not a gifted musician, music can still be helpful in setting an atmosphere in which you can pray. Just choose a worship track and begin to sing and let the worship focus your heart on God. As you allow the worship to stir your love for God it will awaken your desire to pray and then begin to tell God you love Him. So learn to set your atmosphere and expand your prayer.

In the appendix at the back of this book I have also listed other aids to prayer that may help you increase your breadth and depth of prayer. What are your triggers? Identify those triggers and atmospheres that make you come alive and begin to incorporate them into your lifestyle of prayer.

PRAYING BEYOND OUR PERSONALITY

As you consider all these ways to pray you may feel overwhelmed and that your prayer life is very inadequate. But before you disqualify yourself, please remember your ability to pray does not depend just on your natural personality. We have already discussed in chapter one the role of the Holy Spirit to come alongside us to transform and adapt our lives to enable us to pray. I have met many tired prayer warriors, who have ministered out of their sensitive heart for broken people, and have then become overwhelmed by the burden of those people's needs.

Too often we have a wrong understanding of the source of our prayer strength and we think that we need particular types of personality in order to pray well. We assume, "She's an intercessor because she's wired that way – *she is so compassionate.*" I don't believe that your ability to pray is dependent on your personality at all. Your prayer strength flows out of your connectedness with your Father. True prayer is a ministry of love from His heart, through your heart, to others. It is true that some people's personalities are naturally more merciful, but if the source and basis for their prayer is their own personality, before long they will burn out.

PREPARING THE PRAYER VESSEL

As I will share later in this book, in chapter seven, I nearly died in a serious car accident but God saved my life. These near death experiences have a profound effect on your life as you know God has saved you as a result of prayer and so it places a profound gratitude deep within your being. But I also discovered that, even though I had had such an incredible encounter with God and passionately believed in the power of prayer, I still found it hard to have a personal disciplined prayer life.

I wanted to pray for the nations but I remember I would sit in my wheelchair and decide to pray for Zimbabwe and after about five minutes I would run out of prayers. I began to think, "God, what is the matter with me? I want to pray. I'm totally convinced of the power of prayer. So why can't I pray?" One day, as I was crying out to God in my frustration, He clearly spoke to me with the answer: "Rachel," He said, "stop *trying* so hard to pray. Let me touch your heart first and teach you to love." I immediately realized what I had been doing. In my eagerness to pray I was attempting to find the capacity within myself, instead of receiving His supernatural supply of power to help me pray. I was struggling to discipline my life and find a new prayer fluency but God had wanted to help me all along.

CHANGED BY MY OWN PRAYER

So my wheelchair became my training school, and I learnt that even the most incredible encounter with a prayer-answering God is not enough to make you nice! I discovered that God wants to heal the brokenness within our own hearts so that we can be shaped into a vessel of prayer that He can really use. Remember: prayer often changes you first and then your circumstances. As I sought God for the complete healing of my broken legs, He reminded me that He wanted to heal the "crippled" places of my emotional heart before he healed my legs.

Good prayer will always depend on the condition of your heart. We will never succeed in interceding for others unless God touches and heals the stony places of our heart with His compassion first. He teaches us how to identify with the pain of divorce, the trauma of grief and cancer, the emptiness of drug abuse, the heartbreak of a lost childhood, and the devastation of alcohol abuse. When you feel what others are feeling, it does something to your heart; it makes you willing to go to the place of prayer, and sacrifice as you pour out your heart to God until something changes.

During this season in my wheelchair God revealed the hardness of my heart to me. I am a research scientist by profession. I studied Biochemistry at university and worked as a clinical biochemist in the area of hormone research for several years before going into full time ministry. Naturally I have a logical mind that enjoys administration and due process. Consequently I was a very rational, "just get on with it", type of person. I did not have much patience for what I considered to be "needy" people with issues! In fact, the wheelchair was a good learning experience for me, because this very capable, independent person suddenly had to humble herself and ask for help in simple everyday things. God showed me that people are more precious than paper or systems and that compassion is essential for you to be a good prayer warrior. This is something that we all need to learn. Your journey of discovery and shaping will be different from mine, but the outcome will be the same. God wants to teach us to love others and to be compassionate. Compassionate people are people whom God can trust with the secrets of those who are hurting. He knows that we will stand in the gap for them and endure to see their breakthrough.

At the back of this book we have included a section marked Appendix 2, with valuable information that you can use in prayer sessions as you explore the healing of your heart. Here we have included keys and teaching for these areas of prayer counselling.

The Power of a Laid Down Life

A LOOK AT INTERCESSION AND THE PLACE OF FASTING

ANGELS IN AFRICA

I was challenged once again as I listened to the testimony of this missionary. Her eyes sparkled with life as she shared her stories of life in Africa. "I am so grateful for people who pray for me while I am here on the front line; these prayer warriors have literally saved my life!" she explained. She then told us about a time when she was driving home after a meeting out in the bush and her vehicle broke down. It appeared that she had run out of fuel although she had checked the gauge before she left and it had read full. Now alone, on a deserted road, it was rapidly turning dark and this was not a safe area in which to break down. Nervously she got out of the vehicle and wondered what to do next. She was miles away from the nearby town and help. But across the ocean in Germany another older woman woke up and felt the need to pray. Not sure who or what to pray for she walked into her kitchen to make a drink. Whilst waiting for her coffee to brew she glanced at the photos on her fridge and suddenly felt compelled to pray for a particular missionary. As she began to pray, she felt a sense of urgency and started to cry out to God for the life of this woman she did not even know well.

Back in Africa, a group of menacing men had appeared from nowhere with knives and machetes. Grabbing this woman, they demanded the keys to the vehicle or threatened to kill her. The missionary cried out – "God rescue me!" But already, on the other side of the world, the prayer army was in action. This prayer warrior began to pray – "God keep her safe – repair the vehicle. Keep her safe" – even though she had no physical knowledge of the situation. The men tightened their grip and held the knife to the woman whom they had pinned down on the ground. Suddenly the men became agitated and released their grip. They began to shout – and then stood up and ran away. Understanding some of their local dialect, the missionary heard them say to each other: "Did you see the bright light – the shining ones were coming for our soul!" Apparently they had seen tall shining figures and believed them to be spirit powers that could kill them and so they had run in fear.

Back in Germany the prayer warrior was labouring on her knees – "God send your mighty angels – protect this life!" Suddenly she felt a release in her spirit and knew the crisis was over. She would now enjoy her coffee! Back in Africa the missionary got back into her truck, thanking God for the army of angels that had come to her rescue. Looking at the fuel gauge she prayed and started the vehicle and it drove her safely all the way back to the city. The next day she took it to the garage for a check–up and the mechanic told her – "Mama, the fuel gauge is broken and there is no fuel in this vehicle. The tank is totally empty. How did you drive here?" The missionary smiled – she had driven for 5 hours with supernatural fuel! Later, when the prayer warrior connected with the missionary, they exchanged their exciting adventure. The prayer warrior had been feeling she was of little use to God but here, in the secret place of prayer, God had shown her the power of a laid down life, given in prayer for others.

As we press into the place of prayer, we need to realize that if our prayer time only consists of seeking God for our own personal needs, it will soon become very limited. As children of God, we are called to be people of generosity. So our prayer life needs to stretch beyond our own needs and convenience and reflect a heart of sacrifice. At the heart of our prayer, there needs to be the heartbeat of God, not just our personal list of requests. We need to ask God to share His heart of love with us and then we need to echo His priorities on earth as we pray. If your prayer life feels lifeless and stuck, then ask God to invade your prayer times with His heart for others. God wants your prayer life to be fruitful. Let this scripture from Isaiah inspire your prayer times and, where you have felt barren, let God inject your heart with fresh joy in the place of prayer.

> "Sing, barren woman, you who never bore a child; burst into song, shout for joy, you who were never in labour; because more are the children of the desolate woman than of her who has a husband," says the Lord. "Enlarge the place of your tent, stretch your tent curtains wide, do not hold back; lengthen your cords, strengthen your stakes. For you will spread out to the right and to the left; your descendants will dispossess nations and settle in their desolate cities." (Isaiah 54:1-3)

RADICAL LOVERS

There is great power in a laid down life surrendered to God. Jesus demonstrated this by laying down His life for the world. The Bible explains this principle to us in the Gospel of John, chapter 15 and verse 13, "Greater **love** has no one than this: to lay down one's life for one's friends." So if we want to live a radical life of love, we need to learn to give our life away. One of the places where we can regularly practise this sacrificial life is in the place of prayer.

Choosing a life of sacrificial prayer will cost you something. It will confront your independence, challenge your right to sleep, and redefine how you choose to spend your leisure time. True love always has a price tag: although this love is freely given, it is not cheap! Jesus gave His life for your freedom and now we have an opportunity to surrender our life on behalf of others and their needs. God is calling a radical generation of prayer warriors to arise; those who are prepared to pour out their lives on behalf of the broken and who will fight in the secret places to see people walk into their true freedom.

PRAYERLESSNESS

So when we feel the Holy Spirit stirring us to pray for the lost and the broken around us, we need to willingly respond and make time for this responsibility of intercession. We need to realize that delayed obedience is disobedience. But most of us do procrastinate and try to shake off this urgent call to pray. However, we need to recognize that when we do not obey this call to pray, we sin! This is not an optional extra for the super holy club but a request of God to every ordinary believer to play their part in the prayer army of Heaven.

I remember when God challenged my disobedience and constant excuses. I had convinced myself that I did not need to respond to this call to prayer and that other people could and should do this work. After all, I was busy! But one day I read this scripture in 1 Samuel chapter 12 and verse 23 and God nailed me! This scripture reads as follows:

> "Moreover, as for me, far be it from me that I should sin against the LORD by ceasing to pray for you, and I will instruct you in the good and the right way."

Here Samuel describes prayerlessness as sin. Samuel knew he had a responsibility to pray for Saul and says that, if he did not fulfil his duty of prayer, he would be sinning. Suddenly I realized God was not asking me to pray if I felt like it – He was asking me to pray because He desired it. Now I needed to obey!

A FEW CHANGING THE LIFE OF MANY

In times of crisis we need courageous pioneers who will give their life for the greater good of the majority. All through history we have records of such heroes who took great risks for the sake of the nation. During the Second World War, Winston Churchill made a speech where he thanked war heroes for their sacrifice and his quote, "Never was so much owed by so many to so few", has been famous ever since. This quote could also apply to the role of the intercessor. So much is owed by the Church and society to the few intercessors who have stood sacrificially in the place of prayer on behalf of so many lives for generations.

So will you make the choice to give your life away? In Matthew we read:

"For many are called, but few are chosen." (Matt 22:14)

Some theologians say that a more accurate translation of the Greek into our everyday English would be – "Many are called but few position themselves consistently to be chosen"! In other words, we may have been living a passionate, sacrificial life in our youth but today we are no longer making those costly choices that keep us on the cutting edge of sacrifice. We are still called but we are no longer positioning ourselves to pay the price. Intercession is not a gift given to the specially chosen but a privilege available to everyone who will pay the price. So what about you – will you live a life of prayer that touches the unknown and the unlovely?

THE PRAYER OF INTERCESSION

The prayer of intercession is a prayer of generosity. Why? Because at the heart of this prayer is a call that you need to invest time to pray for others. People can tend to think, "Well, I'm not an intercessor. I can't pray for hours and hours on end – that's not my calling." But we often misunderstand this call of intercession. Every man, woman and child is called to be an intercessor because, in essence, intercession is simply praying like Jesus. Intercession is the prayer that stands in the gap; it is the prayer that builds the bridge of hope to the unreached; it is prayer that goes beyond the "me", "mine" and "I" comfort barrier and begins to carry the concerns of God for the people around you. Intercession is prayer that represents the needs of another person, whom you may or may not know, before God. An intercessor is literally one who fills the gap, one who mediates between two parties.

In Numbers 16:48 we see a lovely description of intercession in the person of Phineas. It says:

> "And Phineas stood between the living and the dead and the plague stopped."

Every time you come in intercession, you are standing between the living and the dead. Maybe a friend of yours has a "dead" situation financially and God will ask you to stand in the gap and pray on their behalf to see the curse of debt broken. Or you may need to stand in the gap for someone who needs healing and releasing from the power of sickness. Intercession is a priestly role in which you come before the Lord to represent someone in need, praying that God will act on their behalf because of your cries. The subject and language of your prayer is usually directed by the Holy Spirit as He prompts you to pray.

THE TWO FACES OF INTERCESSION – THE LION AND THE LAMB
As you stand in the gap and pray, you will find that you will express both the compassion of God for the individual but also the cry of warfare against the enemy's plans. Just as God's wrath and God's compassion are two facets of the same perfect Father, so God wants us to represent these "two faces" of His character in this place of intercession – the warrior face of the lion against the enemy, and the compassionate face of the lamb towards the person. Unfortunately,

when we pray, we often wear the wrong face at the wrong time! We roar like a lion against the broken people, and then act like a lamb towards the devil. However, we need to learn to release the sound of the authority of the Lion of Judah to thwart all of the devil's schemes, but demonstrate the kindness of the Lamb of God as we pray for those who have been brutalized by this enemy. We need to use our spiritual weapons of war to disarm the enemy and all his plans but, equally, we then need to pray for blessing and mercy to touch those who have suffered. For example, if you are praying for a broken marriage and you discover that the husband is an alcoholic, you should pray violently against the spiritual powers of alcohol and divorce that want to rob, steal and kill this marriage. You release the sound of warfare against the enemy and his plan to ruin this marriage. But then you come and pray for the husband and the wife as people within this marriage. You ask God to bless them and pray for freedom from every spiritual stronghold in their lives. You surround them by your prayer with peace and forgiveness. You release the roar against the powers of alcoholism but love the person who is trapped by alcoholism. As you pray, you cleanse the wrong spiritual atmosphere over their lives and home and then you release the new atmosphere of peace and love. As intercessors, learn to carry these two faces of God when you pray.

PREPARE THE WAY FOR THE PEOPLE

God is calling His Church back to a rhythm of dedicated prayer and intercession. God watches over your city and streets and He knows those who walk in our neighbourhoods by name and He is concerned for them. Intercession is praying from God's prayer request list. It is choosing to be a prayer partner with Him. God is looking for a people who will bridge the gap and prepare a way for people to come to Him. As intercessors, we need to build a highway that will bring people into contact with the living God.

Isaiah 62:10 says:

> *"Pass through, pass through the gates! Prepare the way for the people. Build up, build up the highway! Remove the stones. Raise the banner for the nations."*

Every prayer we pray is like laying another piece of tarmac on that highway of freedom. Until the prayer is answered, there is a gap between God and the person or situation you are praying about. By our intercession we bridge that gap. Rarely are we able to build the entire highway in one sitting, but as we keep revisiting it, we lay another section of the road. We need to keep praying until the complete highway is established and we see the physical situation shift and break through. We need to realize that, even when we cannot seem to see any results in the natural, our prayer is having effect in the spiritual dimension. Praying time is never wasted time. Each time we pray, something is happening and atmospheres are shifting in the spiritual realm. One day it will break through; suddenly you will see your answer. So, remember, do not give up! Keep praying and build this highway of prayer and then wait and see what will happen because you took time to pray for someone else in their need.

This cry of intercession can be extended to communities as well as individuals. We need to stand in the gap for our neighbours, our region, and our city. As we increase our time in prayer, I believe God will increase our revelation and give us discernment regarding the spiritual powers that are motivating or affecting our cities. Armed with this Holy Spirit revealed information, we can pray more targeted and effective prayers and then have the joy of seeing previously hopeless situations totally turned around. This is the privilege of intercession.

SHAREHOLDERS OF THE TREASURE IN HEAVEN

In 1 Samuel 30:22 onwards we read this account of David with his fighting men after he had recovered his wives, families and all that the

Amalekites had taken from them. The story reads as follows:

> "Then all the wicked and worthless fellows among the men who had gone with David said, 'Because they did not go with us, we will not give them any of the spoil that we have recovered, except that each man may lead away his wife and children, and depart.' But David said, 'You shall not do so, my brothers, with what the LORD has given us. He has preserved us and given into our hand the band that came against us. Who would listen to you in this matter? For as his share is who goes down into the battle, so shall his share be who stays by the baggage. They shall share alike.' And he made it a statute and a rule for Israel from that day forward to this day." (Samuel 30:22-25)

Here we read that David had to confront some of his warrior soldiers who wanted a greater share of the spoils for themselves rather than share with those who stayed with the provisions. They felt they had done the harder work and so deserved a greater reward. However, David does not agree with their way of thinking and immediately stops them. Then in verse twenty-four we read that David outlines the principle of being equal shareholders, whether you fight on the frontlines or stay in the place of provision. David makes it very clear that from God's perspective there is equal value for those who work in the place of prayer and provision and those who work on the frontline with the people. God rewards them both equally!

So when you pray and shift history, or save the life of a missionary in trouble, you need to realize that you are a stakeholder in all they do. You are a shareholder in every breakthrough; you have a share in every life saved and person set free. This is your eternal reward. I have learnt to combat the thoughts of worthlessness or weariness that can overwhelm us with this truth: I am a major stakeholder in the Kingdom of Heaven and no one can ever take this treasure from me.

Proverbs 11:30 says this:

> "The fruit of the righteous is a tree of life, and the one who is wise saves lives."

This is my certificate of promise! I love the amplified version of this scripture too as it emphasises this fact that, when we pray and give our lives to touch others with Jesus, this is part of our reward and a wise investment. So here is the amplified version: "The fruit of the uncompromisingly righteous is a tree of life, and he who is wise captures human lives for God, as a fisher of men – he gathers and receives them for eternity!" So do not hold back and feel that because you "just" pray you are a second class citizen in the church. Prayer warriors are given the same reward as those who fight on the front line of evangelism and missions. So keep changing the world from your front room as God calls you to pray.

HANDLING PRAYER REQUESTS WITH INTEGRITY

Much of our intercessory prayer life is stirred by the numerous prayer requests that cross our path. You may pick up an email informing you of the recent cancer diagnosis of a friend, or the pastor may call you to pray for a couple with marriage problems. You may open the mail and read a magazine article about a missionary adventure, or just pick up the phone and have a call asking you to please pray. In these days of rapid communication, we can quickly become overwhelmed with the constant demand of people's needs. All around us are genuine and critical needs, all asking for our prayer. So how do we handle these requests with both sensitivity and integrity? What is our responsibility to pray?

When people discover that you are a person of prayer they will often ask you to pray for their need. As these requests increase, you need to find a process to select your God given projects from the midst of the pile, with both kindness and discernment. Usually, after I have spoken at a conference, I have numerous people surrounding me, asking me to pray for them and their pressing need. Whenever possible I try to do this instantly with them, right at that moment, and I give them the promise that, if God reminds me to pray further, I will, but otherwise I will just pray this once. I have found people often want to just give you the information to pray but they hesitate to involve themselves in the work of prayer! So I then ask the person to stand with me and pray for their need first before I take the request. Often they ask me to continue to pray and so I will give them my email and ask them to email me with the information and if possible a photo of the person in question. I find that just this request, asking for some engagement on their part, usually cuts down the list by 80%: most people never email me with a follow up of their need and so I feel released from my responsibility. The reason I have developed this method is because I want to keep integrity in my prayer life. If I say I will pray I want to make sure that I will actually pray. Quickly I have realized that I need a process of remembering what I have promised, as I often say – "I will pray for you" – and then immediately forget my promise. So, by asking the individual to be responsible for sending me the information, the ball is in their court and then they are responsible.

Too often I meet wonderful prayer people who are worried by promising too much and praying too little! I think it is vital that you develop a boundary around your intercessory life and ask God for a strategy of knowing when, for whom and how you should pray. Then bring the pile of requests to God and ask Him to show you who He has placed on your prayer list. Once you have selected the prayer requests that the Holy Spirit is asking you to carry to Him in prayer, there are many ways that you can pray for them. However, the heart of identification is always a key. We need to come alongside these people and carry their burden.

YOUR NEED BECOMES MY NEED

I will never forget the first time the Holy Spirit challenged me and taught me this secret of identification. It was during a Sunday morning service in Malaysia. The service had been long, the hall was hot and humid, and I was tired. My baby son, David, had not slept well the night before and I felt irritated and wanted to make sure we left the service very promptly in order to get out of the parking lot before the traffic jam. This was a large church with more than 5,000 people present. As the speaker finished and the worship team stood for the last song, I was up, grabbing my things and encouraging Gordon to move out of our row. But just then the service leader took back the microphone and asked everyone to stand still. I was frustrated. He then asked us to stand and pray for an urgent prayer request they had just received. One of the members of the church had just had to rush their 8 week old baby boy to the hospital. The hospital staff suspected some sort of liver failure and the baby was in a critical condition. We stood still and the church prayed. My prayer was rushed and half-hearted: I was thinking more about my place in the car park queue than this baby boy as I prayed. But in that moment the Holy Spirit rebuked me. "Rachel, would you want this church to pray for David if he was sick in the way you just prayed for this child?" I felt challenged by my lack of compassion. How could I be more concerned about getting my car out of a car park than praying for this little boy who was dying? I was confronted by my selfishness. The Holy Spirit spoke to me again – "Rachel – now pray as if this boy was David – let me teach you to pray with identification – pray as if this was *your* son!"

This encounter with God that Sunday morning impacted the way I pray for prayer requests for the rest of my life. Whenever I pick up a request, I always say to myself – "Now pray as if it is *your* child and *your* life!"

UNDERSTANDING THE KEY OF IDENTIFICATION

Identification is the practical expression of our compassion that positions us to pray alongside people in their pain and circumstances. We know that Jesus modelled this with His life as he was ready to stand with us so that we could then stand with Him. Hebrews 4:15 says of Him:

> "For we do not have a high priest who is unable to sympathise with our weaknesses, but we have one who has been tempted in every way, just as we are – yet was without sin."

This total identification of Jesus with us is also movingly described in the book of Isaiah 53:4-6:

> "Surely he took up our infirmities and carried our sorrows, yet we considered him stricken by God, smitten by him, and afflicted. But he was pierced for our transgressions, he was crushed for our iniquities; the punishment that brought us peace was upon him, and by his wounds we are healed. We all, like sheep, have gone astray, each of us has turned to his own way; and the LORD has laid on him the iniquity of us all."

Here we see Jesus demonstrate the power of identification. Jesus, who knew no sin, became sin. Jesus totally identified with us and stepped out of His world into our world of sin, and, grasping our life, he raised us up to stand with Him in His righteousness. So when you pray for someone who is still gripped by sin, you should not pray with an aloof attitude that keeps you distant from their problem, but you need to pray alongside them in their need with a heart of compassion. This prayer of identification reaches out a hand to a person right where they are, and by your prayers you lift them up to where they should be.

Jesus was tempted in every way that we are tempted, and so this means He understands how we feel when we are tempted. In this same way, we need to allow our emotions to be touched by the pain of others so that we can identify with their needs more easily. The Bible tells us to:

> "Rejoice with those who rejoice, and weep with those who weep". (Romans 12:15 NKJV)

It should not be unusual to see people touched by the Holy Spirit in their emotions as they begin to pray. We will begin to weep for individuals, situations, or even a nation, as we let God teach us to stand with them. In these situations, I believe that God allows us to either feel what He is feeling or what the people themselves are feeling so that we are able to identify with their pain. Either way, this weeping is more than just emotional tears; it is a powerful prayer of identification.

MOSES – A ROLE MODEL

Moses was an incredible intercessor who continually identified himself with his people. I wonder how many pastors would like the opportunity to pastor his church – a church of one million complainers?! For forty years Moses walked with them in the wilderness with nowhere else to go. They frequently threatened to kill Moses; they constantly accused him; they called him a failure and even said that they would prefer to go back and live under the slavery in Egypt than have his leadership. At what must have been one of the lowest points of his ministry, Moses returned from a most amazing encounter with God, where God had spoken to him face to face, and then discovered that, while he had been having this visitation, his leaders had betrayed him and led the people into idol worship. They broke every rule with their sexual sin, pagan festivities and compromise. Events reached a critical point when God said to Moses that he could no longer tolerate their rebelliousness. At this point, after all Moses had endured, you would have expected him to agree with God and say, "Go ahead and let them have what they deserve!" But no, Moses pleaded for his people and cried out, "No, God! Don't do it!" We read this account in Exodus:

> "Then Moses returned to the LORD and said, 'Oh, these people have committed a great sin, and have made for themselves a god of gold! Yet now, if You will forgive their sin – but if not, I pray, blot me out of Your book which You have written.'" (Exodus 32:31-32)

What an amazing response and attitude! Moses so identified with the people of Israel that he said to God, "If you are going to blot these people out, you're going to have to count me out too, because I'm going with them!" Moses so identified with the people he was leading that he said to God – "These people and I are one – God you will have to judge us together!" Could we say that about the people who live in our community, our city, and our nation? "God, if you are going to do something to my neighbourhood then you'll have to do it to me as well, because I am with these people!" What a challenge – what a heart of identification!

Identification is more than sympathy – it is a spiritual connection.

FAST AND PRAY

Why do fasting and prayer go together? I believe it is because prayer is so much more than mere words. Powerful prayer demands more than the language of our mouths: it needs to be combined with the cry from our life too. God uses our actions and attitudes during fasting to come alongside our spoken prayers to expand the breadth and depth of our prayer. Prayer and fasting are so complementary, as together they create an atmosphere of hunger which turns the heart of God towards our longing. When God asks us to fast, he is asking us to exchange our natural appetite for food with a spiritual appetite for Him, and to spend this devoted, defined period of time with Him alone. When we fast we are making a declaration with our life and saying to God, "I hunger for you more than I want my food! I am choosing to put you first!"

Fasting is traditionally understood to be the abstinence from all food for a specific number of days as a dedication to God. Christians are not the only people who include fasting as a sign of their devotion to God. These days we are more aware of the Muslims and their time of fasting over Ramadan, a period of 30 days when devout Muslims will pray and fast as an expression of their religion. As Christians we have largely lost this practice of a regular period of prayer with fasting as part of our lifestyle in the Church, but I believe it is coming back. God is asking His Church to be ready to live a laid down life of true devotion where we will sacrifice and be disciplined. But should we expect fasting to be part of the prayer life of an ordinary Christian?

In Matthew 6:16-18 we read:

> "And when you fast, do not look gloomy like the hypocrites, for they disfigure their faces that their fasting may be seen by others. Truly, I say to you, they have received their reward. But when you fast, anoint your head and wash your face, that your fasting may not be seen by others but by your Father who is in secret. And your Father who sees in secret will reward you."

Immediately we notice in this passage that the Bible uses the word "when" rather than the word "if", implying that there is an assumption that every Christian will fast occasionally. So we ought to accept this fact that, as Christians, we should include regular times of fasting into our lifestyle. We then need to let this scripture teach us about the protocol, behaviour and attitude when we do fast. Fasting can no longer be considered just as an optional extra for the superstar Christian but more as a natural expression of our love for God. So, apart from valid medical reasons which might preclude abstinence from food, we should ask God to show us how to include fasting as part of our way of life.

PREPARING TO FAST

So how should you prepare for a time of fasting?

Remember that the Holy Spirit is a responsible spirit and He will guide and instruct you in the perfect way for you! Before you fast you need to ask God to show you what type of fast you need to do and what should be the length of time. Although fasting is usually considered, in its purest form, to be the discipline of your appetite for food in obedience to God, sometimes God asks us to fast from other consuming appetites. God will challenge the areas of your life in which you may need greater self–control and, for a period of time, He may ask you to "fast" the amount of time you give to your sport, TV, or eating chocolate. Maybe you already know that you waste large amounts of time on a particular activity rather than food and you know it would be good for you to specifically discipline this area for a while. A young man who was ruled by his passion for football once asked me, "I think the Holy Spirit has told me to fast from playing my video games and watching football for a while. Do you think that sounds like God?" I replied, "Yes, if that is an addictive appetite in your life, and God wants to train you, then it sounds like God to me!"

Before you start any period of fasting, especially if it is from food, you need to take some time to prepare yourself. You should always check, with a doctor if necessary, that you are medically fit and able to abstain from food. You may need to check that you can continue taking your medications without food etc. We need to be wise! If you have had issues with eating disorders or are diabetic then fasting from food is probably not the best exercise for you. Ask God to show you an alternative area of life that you can sacrifice in this season. Once you know what you should fast then ask God to show you how to fast. If you do not have an established pattern of fasting from food I would suggest that you do not start with a 40 day fast with water alone. This may kill you! Learning to fast is like learning to run a marathon – you need to take one segment at a time and so build up your stamina slowly but regularly. The training of your appetite and desires takes time. So start by fasting one meal a day and then progress to fasting for a whole 24 hours. You can then build up gradually until you can fast for longer time periods as the Holy Spirit instructs you. Longer fasts of 21 or 40 days need careful planning and usually require that you alter your working schedule so that your body can have some extra rest.

SEASONS OF DEVOTION

Ultimately, fasting is creating space for a special season of devotion to God. It is a time where, by surrendering and disciplining our desires, they in turn become a sacrificial offering to God. But in order to gain the maximum effectiveness from our time of fasting we need to steward any extra time released as a result of not eating, preparing meals, or not watching TV as a dedicated time of extra prayer. The Bible asks us to both "fast and pray"; however we can tend to "fast and play"! But as we learn to connect these times of fasting with times of powerful prayer, something dynamic happens. Suddenly our prayers are connected to an attitude of sacrifice and devotion. This prayer seems to move beyond words into another dimension of intimacy with God and we discover a new authority which resists the enemy.

This is the kind of prayer and fasting that God is calling His Church to participate in. We long to pray, but more than a form of dutiful prayer – we want to pray the kind of prayers that touch Heaven and shift something on earth. This is the time for the Church to find a voice of authority in the place of prayer. So, as we stand on behalf of others and pray, let us learn a new kind of powerful sacrificial prayer that opens up the heavens and sees the power of God released on earth.

Prayer:

Father we ask you today to make us a people of prayer ready to pray effective prayers on behalf of others. We ask you to speak to us and show us how to lay down our lives in the place of prayer for others. Help us deal with our selfishness and train us to have a new discipline in our prayer life. Teach us to consecrate our lives in a new devotion of prayer. Train us to understand your rhythm of prayer for our life in this season. Father we know this is the time for ordinary people to pray extraordinary prayers! So, please take our lives and teach us to pray for our families, neighbours, regions and nations. Thank you for your spirit of prayer resting on our lives. Amen.

Praying with Royal Authority

DECLARATIVE PRAYER AND
ROYAL INTERCESSION

PART OF A ROYAL HOUSEHOLD

In the last chapter we studied the role of the intercessor and the heart of generosity that will stand and pray for another's needs. We looked at the role of a surrendered life and the prayers of intercession that stand in the gap and touch Heaven on behalf of man. But too often we can carry the wrong picture of our role in this place of intercession. In our mind's eye we picture ourselves as the "poor man" pleading with a reluctant God who considers us to be an insignificant nuisance. But when we read the following passage in the first book of Peter, we discover that we are called royal intercessors and we have been given a place of acceptance and authority:

> *"But you are a chosen people, **a royal priesthood**, a holy nation, a people belonging to God, that you may declare the praises of him who called you out of darkness into his wonderful light."*
> *(1 Peter 2:9)*

Here the Bible reminds us that God has chosen us to be His and we are not an irritation to Him. We belong to God and He loves to have communication with us. We enter His presence, not only as priests, but as royal priests. The priest stands before God on behalf of man, and before man on behalf of God. A priest illustrates our role as intercessors. But we are called to be royal intercessors. So what does this ROYAL intercession look like? Too often, when we come to God, we pray with a hesitant, pleading tone, like that of a servant. We approach God like the prodigal son, expecting to be rejected. But God wants us to come and pray as part of the royal priesthood: we should pray out of confidence in our relationship with Him. We need to remember that we have a real relationship with the King and so we should pray with confidence, authority and dignity!

RAISING PRINCES IN THE LAND

Out of this place of intimacy with our Father, who is also the King of Kings, there should emerge a new sound of authority. As we grow in acceptance that God has chosen us, and we are part of His royal household, a new confidence should shape our identity. Intimacy was designed to lead to fruitfulness. When a man and a woman are intimate, the natural result is the birth of a child. In the same way we should expect to see fruitfulness come from our relationship with God: we are designed to bear fruit and multiply! So something needs to come from this place of intimacy in our prayer lives. God has given us the privilege to birth "princes" in the land. In Psalm 45 we read the beautiful description of the King with His princess bride and see the generational legacy that flows from this relationship:

> "All glorious is the princess within her chamber; her gown is interwoven with gold. In embroidered garments she is led to the king; her virgin companions follow her and are brought to you. They are led in with joy and gladness; they enter the palace of the king. Your sons will take the place of your fathers; **you will make them princes throughout the land**. I will perpetuate your memory through all generations; therefore the nations will praise you forever and ever." (Psalm 45:13-17)

So we have this privilege, as His royal intercessors, to birth a new legacy as we pray. God is calling the Church to enter the secret place and birth princes throughout the land. We need a fresh revelation of our royal lineage so that we can enter the inner courts of the King and reverse the effects of poor leadership in our nations. It is time to raise princes in the land. We need to mentor and protect the next generation, and by our authoritative prayer make a way for them to be released into their governmental roles in our nations. We are not only priests who can petition but we are also royalty who have the authority to issue edicts and decrees. As we begin to grasp the privilege of our relationship in the place of prayer, we will start to declare the vision of His Kingdom. We will encourage the prophetic dreamers and urge them to pray for breakthrough. We will learn to recognize our jurisdiction in the spirit and then govern in it. This is the time to raise people of influence for the nations. We carry His royal DNA and so we should expect to be raising the history makers, the nation shapers, the reformers and entrepreneurial people. Many brave people run in our family line so we should get ready to birth pioneers and people of great courage. It is time to raise princes in our nations!

SECURE IN MY ROYAL IDENTITY

If we are going to be people who pray with a Kingdom mind-set, then we must learn to pray from a secure position as part of the royal household of Heaven. Right now the Church is in a season of preparation: it is time for the Church to grow in confidence in her royal identity and prepare her ways of thinking and speaking as a royal bride. In the book of Revelation we read:

> "Let us rejoice and be glad and give him glory! For the wedding of the Lamb has come, **and his bride has made herself ready**." (Revelation 19:7)

The Bible announces in this passage that the bride is ready for Heaven, and the work in her heart has been completed. Throughout the Church there has been an emotional poverty spirit. Most people do not believe that God has made them valuable or significant. In fact, we tend to judge those who seem too secure as arrogant. But it is so important that we have a correct "God view" of who we are and what we are called to accomplish. Too often we underestimate His call in the name of humility but God wants us to treasure the gifts He has given us and to use them to make His name great. Do you see yourself as significant, able to accomplish your call, and designed to perfectly work with God?

REJECTION IS DECEPTION

We need to recognize where the enemy has blocked up the wells of our emotions and damaged our ability to receive and accept that we are loved. The Philistines, a picture of the enemy, come into the wellspring of our heart and fill it with mud. Let us read this passage in Genesis:

> "So all the wells that his father's servants had dug in the time of his father Abraham, the Philistines stopped up, filling them with earth." (Genesis 26:15)

Because of this "mud", so many of our emotional responses have been blocked up and so we struggle to believe that we are loved. We live in fear of rejection from everyone and especially God. We have swallowed the lie that we have little value and that people endure, rather than enjoy, our company. But the absolute central core of who God is – is love. God is completely committed and loves everything that He has made. So rejection is the greatest lie as it contradicts the very nature of God. REJECTION IS DECEPTION and the Church must shake free from all its insecurity and allow the Holy Spirit to give it such a revelation of His incredible love!

Too often we have believed the lie that we are not good enough. We have worn the labels that proclaim – "I am a failure – I have no friends – I am too fat etc." But we need to have a revelation – I am His royal child!

CLOTHED WITH STRENGTH AND DIGNITY

Do you understand whose you are? You carry royal blood and destiny in your veins. You are born into a royal household and you are being trained for a throne! We read about this beautiful bride in Proverbs 31:

> *"She is clothed with strength and dignity; she can laugh at the days to come." (Proverbs 31:25)*

You have been chosen to wear a crown of dignity. Jesus took the crown of thorns, the crown of rejection, so that we could wear the crown of splendour and acceptance. We are not an accident; we are individually and personally hand crafted for purpose by the greatest creator and perfectly fitted for our function.

If you are ever to truly pray, exercising your full authority, then you must break the lie of all negativity and walk like His royal child, comfortable to wear your crown. This crown is worn on your head, surrounding your mind with your royal status as a child of the King. As you wear this crown, let it destroy every stronghold of "stinking thinking" that lodges in your mind and begin to declare: "I am a child of the King of Kings!" You need to realize that what you feel is not your true reality: it is what is carried within you, all your dreams, talents and aspirations – this is your spiritual DNA and your true life. All the potential of your yet unspoken dreams and the visions for your life – this is who you truly are. But will you let what is on the inside of you stand up boldly and be displayed, so that all can see it? It is time for the people of God, unashamed of all the strengths and talents given to them by God, to be revealed so that everyone can see them. Let the royal bride of great beauty and strength be revealed.

BORN FOR PURPOSE

This is an Esther hour for the Church in many nations and it is not the time for the royal bride to remain silent. Like Queen Esther we have been born for this season with a purpose for this hour. We must realize the privilege of the opportunity that God has given to us at this time and be confident of our royal mandate. We must speak out against injustice; we must not compromise our God given standards, and we must fulfil our leadership roles with great wisdom! It is the time for the Church to lead its nation and people with dignity. In the book of Esther we read this passage:

> "Mordecai sent back this answer: 'Do not think that because you are in the king's house you alone of all the Jews will escape. For if you remain silent at this time, relief and deliverance for the Jews will arise from another place, but you and your father's family will perish. And who knows but that you have come to royal position for such a time as this?' Then Esther sent this reply to Mordecai: 'Go, gather together all the Jews who are in Susa, and fast for me. Do not eat or drink for three days, night or day. I and my maids will fast as you do. When this is done, I will go to the king, even though it is against the law. And if I perish, I perish.' So Mordecai went away and carried out all of Esther's instructions." (Esther 4:13-17)

Esther was reminded that her privileged position also demanded that she take responsibility. Mordecai confronted Esther and reminded her that she should not just enjoy living in the king's household but she needed to use this place of influence as a platform for justice. He challenged her that she should not remain silent at this critical time for her people but she needed to take time in prayer and fasting for the sake of her nation. Esther heard the rebuke – "Do not hold back!" – and she responded, knowing it could cost her everything, including her life.

We, too, have a royal mandate from Heaven. There is a job for us to do and we need to stand up boldly, walk with dignity, and fulfil what we have been asked to do in this day in our nations. We are a royal priesthood – so now let us pray and fast on behalf of our nation and reverse every curse the enemy has planned. It is time for royal intercession.

PRAYER OF DECLARATION

Royal intercession is a prayer that has a stronger, more authoritative, sound. It speaks and declares as an ambassador of God. We see this in Jesus' life when a boy who was demon possessed was brought to Him. Jesus prayed a simple prayer of proclamation, "Be delivered!", and the boy was set free. When Jesus met the blind man who wanted to see, He commanded his blind eyes to, "Be opened!", and they were. Then, when Jesus stood up in the disciples' boat while they were still in the midst of the storm, He simply decreed, "Peace. Be still.", and the water calmed. This prayer tends to speak with an authority from Heaven addressing a situation on the earth. So it sounds and uses a different language from our usual supplicative or asking prayer, but this prayer is one which, I believe, God wants us to understand and use more in these days. Often, after times of personal prayer, we will find that the Holy Spirit will reveal a situation to us and then give us words to declare that confront the issue and bring freedom.

A PRAYER THAT CARRIES POWER

Several years ago now, I was in a women's conference in Norway when a lady was brought into the back of the meeting. Someone came to the front and grabbed me and took me to this woman saying, "Please, come and pray for her." I looked at her and vaguely recognized her, and then realized she was a friend. She looked weak and desperately sick – in fact so ill that I could hardly recognize her.

My friend was lying on a couch and struggled to lift her head to speak to me. As I looked at her tired body, I prepared myself to pray with her in a gentle and compassionate style, but suddenly, before I could stop myself, I felt a loud cry of indignation rise up in me and I declared at the top of my voice, "No! You will not die! This sickness has got to stop now!" This prayer was spoken with such authority and force that I was totally surprised by it, but I knew deep down that this cry had been stirred by the Holy Spirit and I was just His mouthpiece. This process repeated itself several times. As I tried to pray a more pastoral prayer, suddenly a shout of declaration erupted from my mouth and I found myself shouting "No" as I looked at the curse of this sickness on her body. The Holy Spirit then touched her body and she began to vibrate all over. I watched her for a while but she did not seem to respond or be able to speak, so I excused myself as I needed to visit the bathroom after a long service, but when I returned she had gone. I was disappointed not to be able to talk to her and concerned that I could have offended her with my loud prayer.

However, about two weeks later, the phone rang at my home in England and it was this friend. She had been healed, her strength had returned, and she was out of her bed and eating. God had touched her body and delivered her from this sickness. Through this strong declarative prayer that did not sound particularly nice or polished, God had spoken His word and touched her body. I believe that we need to carry this sound of royal declaration and watch the power of our prayer increase.

PATTERNS FROM THE PRAYER LIFE OF JESUS

Unfortunately we cannot just adopt a tone or simple formula and then apply it rigidly and get perfect results every time we pray. If you study the life of Jesus, you will discover that, although Jesus had a definite rhythm to His prayer life, there was no prescriptive formula. His prayer life consisted of a balance between more intimate devotional times with God, followed by more declarative times of public prayer. But by watching the way Jesus spent time in the private prayer place the disciples' curiosity was stirred and, after one such time, they approached Jesus and asked Him to teach them to pray. We read this account in Luke 11:

> *"One day Jesus was praying in a certain place. When he finished, one of his disciples said to him, 'Lord, teach us to pray, just as John taught his disciples.'" (Luke 11:1)*

The disciples watched Jesus pray and it stirred in them a hunger to learn a new depth of prayer. They had seen Jesus withdraw and pray alone in remote spaces and then return and flow with power, miracles and healing in the public place. They wanted to learn this secret of His balance of private and public prayer.

JESUS TOOK TIME TO PRAY

Although we do not have any actual content or defined structure from the prayer times of Jesus, we do know that Jesus carved out time to pray. Through the following scriptures we are able to gain some insight into His prayer life. Here are some of the scriptures that relate to these times of prayer:

> *"Very early in the morning, while it was still dark, Jesus got up, left the house and went off to a solitary place, where he prayed." (Mark 1:35)*

> *"But Jesus often withdrew to lonely places and prayed." (Luke 5:16)*

> *"He withdrew about a stone's throw beyond them, knelt down and prayed." (Luke 22:41)*

> *"And being in anguish, he prayed more earnestly, and his sweat was like drops of blood falling to the ground." (Luke 22:44)*

Immediately we can see that Jesus made sure His times of prayer were in a place and at a time when he was focussed and undistracted. He chose the early mornings, went to lonely places, and withdrew from people. His private times of prayer were earnest and intentional. He definitely created space to pray within His schedule and chose somewhere where he could pray without interruption.

But what is exciting to note is that, when Jesus left these times of prayer, the next verses record that mighty miracles started to happen. In Mark 1:35 we read that Jesus is in prayer but He comes out of this prayer place with POWER! We read the account of what happens in the next verses:

> *"So he travelled throughout Galilee, preaching in their synagogues and driving out demons. A man with leprosy came to him and begged him on his knees, 'If you are willing, you can make me clean.' Filled with compassion, Jesus reached out his hand and touched the man. 'I am willing', he said. 'Be clean!' Immediately the leprosy left him and he was cured." (Mark 1:39-42)*

Again in Luke 5:16 Jesus has been praying alone, in the secret place, but when he finishes his time of prayer He comes out into His community and heals the sick. We read about this a few verses later in the same chapter of Luke:

> *"Immediately he stood up in front of them, took what he had been lying on and went home praising God. Everyone was amazed and gave praise to God. They were filled with awe and said, 'We have seen remarkable things today.'" (Luke 5:25-26)*

PRIVATE PRAYER – THE INTIMATE TIME WITH THE FATHER

Before Jesus left His disciples on earth, He instructed them to learn how to wait and receive power in the place of prayer. We read this in Luke chapter 24 as follows:

> "I am going to send you what my Father has promised; but stay in the city until you have been clothed with power from on high." (Luke 24:49)

Jesus declares that He is going to His Father and that He will send us a promised gift of power. We have already discussed earlier, in chapter one of this book, the principle of knowing that we are a friend of God and the role of the Holy Spirit in helping us to access this truth. Too often we want to demonstrate the power of God without taking the time to invest in our relationship with Him. Jesus spent time with His Father. In the midst of a busy and demanding ministry, when everyone was pressing Him with their needs, Jesus learnt how to withdraw from people and connect with His Father. We need to understand that, unless we make time to download from God, we will have no power to transfer. If you study the life of the Desert Fathers, or the ancient mystics, you find they understood a rhythm of life that was more contemplative and intimate. They describe in their writings how they accessed the secrets of Heaven and understood the principles of "waiting on God". In today's busy society we too often use a "drive through" mentality when we come into the presence of God. We give our prayer order at the counter of Heaven and then expect to collect the answer a few minutes later! However, we need to learn the art of lingering in the presence of God. We should take time and practise renewing our mind and ways of thinking. We must wait and absorb the atmosphere of Heaven and listen to what God is saying. In this private place of prayer we need to give God an opportunity to shape our priorities and ways of thinking and then give us revelation. This place of private prayer is where God changes us so that we can go out and then change the world.

PUBLIC PRAYER – CARRYING A MESSAGE FROM GOD

As we leave this place of private prayer we should go out knowing that we have received a word from Heaven, not just a "nice" idea. We need to carry a specific message from the heart of the Father for the people we meet. In the Gospel of Matthew, Jesus instructs His disciples to go out and carry good news and so we read:

> *"As you go, preach this message: 'The kingdom of Heaven is near.' Heal the sick, raise the dead, cleanse those who have leprosy, drive out demons. Freely you have received, freely give." (Matthew 10:7-8)*

Here in this scripture, Jesus instructs His disciples to go and bring the reality of Heaven closer to people's lives. So, as we speak our God-given message, we ought to realize that we, too, reveal the Kingdom of Heaven to people in trouble. As we go, we should proclaim this message to those around us who need hope, and demonstrate that God is neither remote nor uncaring. We must help them break the cycles of fear and encourage them with this good news: God can heal the sick and raise the dead; He can deliver from torment and set people free. God is able to totally forgive, make you feel clean and give you a new life. This is the message we are called to carry and, as we speak out this good news, Heaven draws close to people. They find real life again. All through the life of Jesus we can observe this rhythm of private prayer followed by periods of miraculous power being released and people being touched. This was the pattern of His supernatural life.

PRAY LIKE THE EARLY CHURCH

Most of us want to see our churches grow, our friends saved, and witness signs and miracles like those in the Early Church, but we are not so eager to pay the price to pray or endure their persecution! But as you study the book of Acts, you discover that this Early Church was a church that knew the power and discipline of prayer.

In Acts 2:42 we read:

> "They devoted themselves to the apostles' teaching and to fellowship, to the breaking of bread and to prayer."

This church was intentional about spending quality time in prayer. But then you notice that, like Jesus, after their times of prayer, there were amazing outbreaks of miracles. In Acts chapter 3 we read about Peter and John healing the lame man at the temple gate:

> "Then Peter said, 'Silver or gold I do not have, but what I do have I give you. In the name of Jesus Christ of Nazareth, walk.'" (Acts 3:6)

Once again, out of the place of prayer, a supernatural healing occurred. We could be forgiven for thinking that the obvious next stage for this church would be popularity and fame. But instead of celebrating these healings, the community leaders became jealous and suspicious and began to oppose this Early Church. So in Acts chapter 4 we read that the local leaders began to persecute the church.

> "The priests and the captain of the temple guard and the Sadducees came up to Peter and John while they were speaking to the people. They were greatly disturbed because the apostles were teaching the people, proclaiming in Jesus the resurrection of the dead. They seized Peter and John and, because it was evening, they put them in jail until the next day. But many who heard the message believed; so the number of men who believed grew to about five thousand." (Acts 4:1-4)

So what was the response of this fledgling church? Did they tone down their message and become more culturally sensitive? No – this persecution did the opposite and only stirred them to increase their level of prayer! They did not withdraw from the situation but retreated into God and began to pray with passion.

We read:

> *"When they heard this, they raised their voices together in prayer to God. 'Sovereign Lord', they said, 'you made the heavens and the earth and the sea, and everything in them.'"* (Acts 4:24)

It is interesting that they are not asking God to get them out of their tough situation: they are asking God to give them more boldness and authority to walk through this season of opposition without fear. Their answer to the persecution was MORE prayer! Once they had finished praying they then returned to the streets and did not hide. In fact, they performed more miracles with more power. We read in Acts:

> *"The apostles performed many signs and wonders among the people. And all the believers used to meet together in Solomon's Colonnade."* (Acts 5:12)

So we read that more prayer led to more power but also to more persecution. Here again the leaders are not happy with what was happening:

> *"Then the high priest and all his associates, who were members of the party of the Sadducees, were filled with jealousy."* (Acts 5:17)

Here we see a pattern, both from the life of Jesus and the Early Church: more prayer leads to more supernatural power released, but this comes with the reaction of hostile opposition too. We can feel that if only we revealed more of the power of God we would have a greater acceptance by the leaders in our communities. Unfortunately both the Bible and Church history would disagree with this theory. In fact, life shows that when the Church prays and then carries more miraculous power, it is usually persecuted by the government. However, then it thrives and becomes more supernatural!

SEND THE WORD

Just as the Early Church prayed and responded, so too we have the privilege to speak a message from the throne room of Heaven and shape history. There is power released when we send a word that comes from Heaven. In Psalm 107:20 we read:

"He sent forth his word and healed them; he rescued them from the grave".

Here we see that God sends His word and within the sound of that Word is the power to heal disease and rescue people from death! So what is the power hidden in this Word? To further understand the power of God's Word in our mouth we probably need to look deeper into some of the science that explains the principles of sound and the way created matter resonates.

Now for a science lesson where I will try to explain in simple terms the formation and resonance of matter. (This will not be technically perfect so if you are an expert in this field I am sorry if you feel I have butchered this concept of pure physics.) So, let us now investigate matter further and break it down into its smallest component parts. Firstly we begin by looking at atoms, which consist of smaller particles called neutrons, electrons and protons with which we are more familiar. However, these days physicists agree that there are even smaller elementary particles called quarks. A quark (/'kwork/ or /'kwark/) can be defined as an elementary particle and a fundamental constituent of matter. Quarks combine together to form hadrons, the most stable of which are called protons and neutrons, which become the component parts of all atomic nuclei. So, at the heart of all atoms are quarks. However, on further examination a quark is not strictly physical matter but a particle carrying a resonance or frequency of sound. In other words it is a sound vibration of a specific frequency for that individual piece of matter. In simple terms, at the heart of every particle of matter there are sound vibrations that are resonating. Matter consists of sound!

So why is all this detail relevant? Let us return to the book of Genesis to answer this question. Genesis describes creation as being formed as a result of the Word of God. It describes how God sent a word – "Let there be light!" and the world was created by this sound and day and night were formed. Each time God created the next stage of the universe, He spoke and then creation resonated with this Word and matter was formed. So at the heart of creation is sound. But this is not just any sound – this is the sound of the voice of God. The Voice of God spoke, particles began to resonate with the sound of this Word and then matter was formed. In Colossians 1:17 we read that God created all things and He continues to uphold all things by His Word. So now let us take a moment to think about how this may apply to the power and effectiveness of the sound of our prayer.

POWERFUL SOUND WAVES

We are all familiar with the principle of an opera singer hitting a high note with perfect pitch and then shattering a wine glass as she sings. If it is possible to use this spoken sound in the natural realm to bring change then just imagine the power of using the Word of God to shift and create in the spiritual domain. Solid glass just shatters at the sound of a trained operatic voice. In a similar way, impregnable circumstances must yield when the Word of God is released by people trained in the place of prayer. We are also familiar with the technique of ultrasound where we target kidney or gall bladder stones with sound waves to disperse the stones and bring healing to the body. These ultrasound waves are programmed to be a specific frequency so that when they hit the stone they resonate at the exact vibration and so the sound shatters the stones. As we listen in the place of prayer, God has the perfect words, at the right frequency, which He wants to give to us so that we can send His word to destroy cancer tumours and disease. God is calling us to send forth His word, like these ultrasonic signals, and watch His word shatter sickness. But we need to train our ears to listen and then release this Word with perfect pitch so that it hits its mark.

There is also another perfect illustration of the power of sound being released as "sound warfare" in the natural. When an army unit approaches a bridge marching in perfect step, the order will be given to break step before they walk onto the bridge. If the soldiers do not break their step and continue marching in unison, the sound of their marching, in perfect step and rhythm, could start a strong vibration that resonates with the structure of the bridge and causes it to collapse! The sound of this army walking in perfect unison could destroy a heavy reinforced concrete bridge! How much more should we expect to carry a spiritual sound which devastates the enemy's strongholds when we unite in spirit and purpose and then speak? This was the discipline which the people of God learned when they marched around the walls of Jericho. The city was tightly shut up but God trained the people under Joshua's command to wait on Him for the right battle cry which, when released at the perfect time, would bring deliverance. We read this story in Joshua chapter 6 below:

> "¹Now the gates of Jericho were securely barred because of the Israelites. No one went out and no one came in. ²Then the Lord said to Joshua, 'See, I have delivered Jericho into your hands, along with its king and its fighting men. ³March around the city once with all the armed men. Do this for six days. ⁴Have seven priests carry trumpets of rams' horns in front of the ark. On the seventh day, march around the city seven times, with the priests blowing the trumpets. ⁵When you hear them sound a long blast on the trumpets, have the whole army give a loud shout; then the wall of the city will collapse and the army will go up, everyone straight in'...¹⁰But Joshua had commanded the army, 'Do not give a war cry, do not raise your voices, do not say a word until the day I tell you to shout. Then shout!'...¹⁶The seventh time around, when the priests sounded the trumpet blast, Joshua commanded the army, 'Shout! For the Lord has given you the city! ¹⁷The city and all that is in it are to be devoted to the Lord.'"
> (Joshua 6:1-5, 10, 16-17)

Here we read of the power of releasing the right sound at the right time to bring down strongholds. The people of Israel were using their "sound" of unity as their weapon of war! This "sound warfare" was all the more powerful as all the people worked together and were of one heart and one spirit, all united in a single purpose and mission. Psalm 133 reminds us that where God's people are together in unity, there God commands a special blessing. There is a unique authority that comes upon the Church when we declare God's word from a place of unity. So God is asking us if we will be a people ready to carry His decrees, with royal authority, and release His creative power to bring change. Are we ready to carry His powerful sound warfare?

Prayer:

So, Father today we consecrate our mouths to you for your service. Let our words be powerful in your hands. Train us to speak with your authority and dignity. We want to be those who no longer carry an attitude of negativity but who carry the healing sound of your Word. Let our lives and words resonate with your power. Help us to connect to you in a deeper way and so change our community with your powerful words of life. Amen.

Breakthrough Prayer

THE PRAYER OF FAITH AND SPIRITUAL WARFARE

FIGHT A GOOD FIGHT

The house was quiet again, the breakfast rush was finished, and the kids were at school. But my mind was full of anxious thoughts. My daughter was facing many challenges: the pull of popularity and severe peer pressure. We were struggling to keep her from making poor choices and again breakfast had been a battlefield. My kids loved Jesus and were part of church but the fight for their affections in these teenage years had been declared! Fear gripped my heart as I began to let horror stories of other teenagers fill my imagination. But suddenly God interrupted my panic and spoke to me – "Fight the good fight of FAITH (1 Tim 6:12) – engage and battle for them."

We want to see breakthrough in the lives of those we love but we often hesitate to declare and battle for their freedom. But, as we studied in the last chapter, we have been called to carry God's word in our mouths and we need to release His written decrees with authority. We have to take His word as the sword of the spirit and be ready to engage in battle. But remember: this is a battle we are destined to win! So do not fear and do not hold back your sound.

115

WINNING THE SPIRITUAL BATTLE FOR LIFE

Spiritual warfare is about bringing the alignment of Heaven and earth into reality in your world. It is taking the promises of God and declaring them into the impossibility of your circumstances. There is a big difference between the facts and the truth. We need to use the word of God, which is the Sword of the Spirit (Ephesians 6:17-18), and declare the truth of God until the facts of our circumstances come into alignment with the promise of God to us. Immediately I began to remember the promises of God which I had received over the years for Nicola and began to speak them out. The word of God in our mouths has power to break the stronghold of fear and imagination that can grip our minds. (2 Corinthians 10:3-5) The "mama bear" had woken up and, as I began to pray, rehearsing the promises of God over my daughter's life, peace returned and a sense of purpose filled my heart. I found myself praying: "I did not give birth to my kids for the devil – I birthed them for the purposes of God. They belong to HIM!" Faith was sealed in my heart that day as I realized it was a battle, but one that God was fighting with me.

There continued to be many such sessions of this intense prayer when I had to hold fast to God's decree over my children's lives. Today both my kids are married to outstanding partners and they love Jesus and are building the next generation for God. In every area of our life – our marriage, workplace, finances, relationships and decisions – we will encounter opposition at some stage, and we need to understand what to do in this season and how to win. Spiritual life in this "stretched out zone" is not easy. You are standing with the knowledge of God's promise on the one hand but with the reality of nothing shifting and the pressure mounting on the other. The battle has been declared!

INTELLIGENT BATTLE STRATEGY

So how do we engage in this battle and win without getting exhausted?

1. **Identify the real issues – (Ephesians 6:10-13)** Do not get distracted by people and their agendas but ask God to show you the enemy's plan and identify how he wants to rob, steal and kill your promise. Fight the right battle and do not make it personal.

2. **Engage in the battle – (Nehemiah 4:13-14)** Ignoring the battle will not make it disappear. We need to speak to the storm! Sometimes we have the attitude, "if I do not bother the devil then he will not bother me", but we need to recognize the battle and engage. We are given authority to use God's Word to resist and rebuke the schemes of the enemy.

3. **Rehearse the truth – (Psalm 149:6-9)** Ask God to give you the right scriptures and to remind you of His promises for this situation and declare these specific words during the days of battle. Let His word in your mouth be a double-edged sword – this word has power against the enemy's plan and also the power to set you free from fear and anxiety. It has double power!

4. **Be happy – (1 Thessalonians 5:16-24)** Keep the right atmosphere around you in this time of battle. We are called to be the happy people with good news even in tough times! Ask God to give you an attitude of gratitude. Remember it is the JOY of the Lord that is our strength and we need this strength in times of struggle! So when you pray, do not whine to God about the difficulties but speak to the obstacle with a confidence that God will help you press through. All prayer should be mixed with thanksgiving – even our prayer of warfare!

THE PRAYER OF FAITH

In these days of fashionable spirituality we find that many different types of people are happy to pray. However, God especially delights to answer the prayer of faith. So we need to understand this dynamic of faith in our prayer lives. In Romans we read:

> "Consequently, faith comes from hearing the message, and the message is heard through the word of Christ. But I ask: 'Did they not hear?'" (Romans 10:17-18).

From this passage it is clear that hearing the message and acquiring faith are linked together. So, if our hearing is defective, our faith will also be limited. In order to have a productive prayer life we need to be confident of our hearing ability in the Spirit. God loves to speak to His children; this is our privilege.

We have already spent a fair amount of time discussing the place of listening and waiting on God as part of our rhythm of prayer. But unless we develop an assurance that we are hearing right, we will not believe that we are carrying His message. So when we then come to pray for people, we will hold back, fearing that they will not experience His supernatural power. We need to believe we have heard God and then speak out boldly! We need to come to the place of faith that what we are hearing is the Word of God for the situation, and then we need to engage in prayer and declare this word with a bold authority, confident that it is a promise of God that will break through with power. This is the prayer of faith.

MAKING A GOOD CONFESSION

So what does a prayer of faith sound like? Basically, it is hearing what God is saying about the situation and then proclaiming this revelation to be the truth in the difficult circumstances. For example, if you hear that your friend has cancer, first go to God and pray, and ask for a word. Once you hear God speak to you, take this promise and pray it into existence. Praying the prayer of faith is making a good confession. In both the book of Romans and 1 Timothy the Greek word *homologeo* is translated as "good confession" in our English Bibles. But if we look at the literal translation of this Greek word, *homologeo*, we find that *homo* means "the same as" and *logeo* or *logos* means "the word of God". So when we read the following scripture in the book of Timothy: "*Fight the good fight of the faith. Take hold of the eternal life to which you were called and about which you made **the good confession** in the presence of many witnesses.*" (1 Timothy 6:12 ESV), we could translate this phrase "the good confession" as "say the same thing as God is saying". In other words this verse would read: "Fight the good fight of the faith. Take hold of the eternal life to which you were called and about which *you say the same thing as God is saying* in the presence of many witnesses."

As we stand to fight this fight of faith, we align our mouths with the mouth of God and we declare His promises in the midst of all the impossibility and proclaim it as God's truth. We need to say what God is saying in the midst of the crisis and not rehearse our doubts and fears. As royal intercessors we have been before God and heard His word, but now we take this word and use it in battle and birth the breakthrough of His promise.

HOLD FAST TO YOUR PROMISES

I believe one of the greatest areas of challenge in our Christian faith is this ability to hold fast and see the reality of God's promises in our lives. It takes great courage to stand in faith and believe when every circumstance is screaming the opposite facts to what you know in your spirit should be your reality. But God wants to remind you today – do not turn back from your promised land! Often we abandon the field of our prayers because the harvest seems so delayed that we believe it will never manifest. So we stop praying for the issue and neglect it and walk away. But God's seed never fails. It will produce a harvest but we must not give up. We forget that not every harvest can be reaped within a few months; some crops take years to mature before they can be harvested. Recently God asked me the question – "What legacy do you want to leave, Rachel? Do you want to leave a bean sprout or an oak tree?" I immediately realized that different legacies will require different times before harvest. A bean sprout grows quickly but, once harvested, rots fast too! But an oak tree takes years before it matures but then it stands the test of centuries and graces the landscape for years. An acorn may not look like much in the beginning but, if it is given time and care, it will produce a legacy for centuries. God is asking us to make long term investments in the place of prayer and we need to trust Him to give us a great harvest.

In the waiting time we need to guard our hearts. There are times when we do need to sow in tears before we can reap with joy. But we need to be encouraged by this promise:

> *"Those who sow in tears will reap with songs of joy. He who goes out weeping, carrying seed to sow, will return with songs of joy, carrying sheaves with him." (Psalm 126:5-6)*

We do not like to hear the first part but it is true – there are often tears of travail and desperation before the happy tears of joy. While we wait for the breakthrough in one field of life, we need to continue to sow more prayer for other needs. We must not allow the time of delay to produce any bitterness that will grip our heart during this waiting time. It is so easy to withdraw our trust, our time, and commitment during times of delay. This is a place where God tests our hearts. In this place of tears God stretches us. We need to realize that, when it feels like we have reached the end, it is never really the end, and God always makes a way in the wilderness. There is a season for everything under the sun – there is a time to sow and a time to reap. We do just have to wait for our appointed time.

So take courage and wait. Your prayers have a designated time for breakthrough. Do not abandon them in hopelessness but keep watering them with your faith and watch and see what God will do for you!

BREAKTHROUGH – A DEFINITION

What do I mean when I use this term "breakthrough"? We may all have different understandings of what we mean by this word. My understanding of a spiritual breakthrough is this:

- It is the sudden release of God's promise into reality from the spiritual realm.
- An occurrence that removes an obstacle withholding your promise.
- A divine strategy that enables you to overcome the enemy's plan and take back ground
- A revelation that accelerates further progress on your path of destiny.

An actual dictionary definition of the word BREAKTHROUGH is: to progress with the development; to advance and progress; to find and keep finding new ways of stepping forward. Breakthrough will release an entrepreneurial spirit of invention, improvement and discovery. Breakthrough will help you leap forwards, turn around events, and take a quantum leap towards your God given calling. This is the more literal everyday meaning of the word.

However, it is interesting to note that the original meaning of this word carried more the sense of discovering the hidden talents and gifts rather than a negative emphasis on removing obstacles and limitations. So maybe there are keys of breakthrough in celebrating the provision of God, rather than just identifying the hindrances in our way. Perhaps we need to turn on the "lights" of God's promises and celebrate Him, rather than be too distracted by the surrounding darkness.

FIND STRENGTH FOR THE LONG HAUL

God spoke to me one morning and said that supernatural grace and favour were being released in these days upon the prayer movements for breakthrough but that we needed to endure and find strength in God. We need to encourage one another and read stories of past breakthroughs so that we stay focussed on our task. I love this promise in Romans:

> "For everything that was written in the past was written to teach us, so that through **endurance** and the encouragement of the Scriptures we might have hope. May the God who gives **endurance** and encouragement give you a spirit of unity among yourselves as you follow Christ Jesus." (Romans 15:4-5)

In this passage the Greek word that is translated as endurance in our English Bibles is the word *hupomone* (hoop-om-on-ay'). Often when we think of the meaning of "endurance" we have a picture of gritted teeth, struggle, and a dogged determination that is just about hanging on until the end of the race. But this word *hupomone* has a much happier tone. This endurance comes from a supernatural source (hupa) that keeps a cheerful and hopeful heart while waiting with a consistent and patient attitude. This supernatural endurance should have a happy attitude as it waits. This endurance is not the gritted determination of our strength of character but it is a deep sense of trust mixed with joy that can sing and declare "I know my God and I believe that He will save me"!

WEARY WARRIORS ARISE!

If you have grown weary in your prayer battle – take courage. Many of us grow weary, not because we have been praying the wrong things, but just because we have been doing the RIGHT things in the RIGHT place for a LONG time and the battle has been very fierce. It is perfectly normal to become weary but we just need to make sure that we do not stay weary. After all, the Bible tells us that:

> *"Even youths grow tired and weary, and young men stumble and fall"* *(Isaiah 40:30).*

So do not beat yourself up if you feel overwhelmed – even youths will get tired! Just allow your strength to be renewed. We all know this promise in Isaiah but sometimes we miss the simple truth:

> *"He gives strength to the weary and increases the power of the weak".* *(Isaiah 40:29)*

Did you know God has a GIFT of strength for you? God GIVES fresh strength to the weary. All we need to do is position ourselves to receive this strength. So take a moment and ask God to refresh you in the battle and receive strength to endure and, finally, break through. Here is one of my favourite scriptures that I love to pray when I am in the midst of a battle. I just use it to thank God again and again that He is my source and resource, right in the gates of the battle zone, and that He will strengthen me to endure and together we will break through! As you read this verse, claim it for your life and situation right now, and let the power of this promise encourage you today!

> *"In that day the LORD Almighty will be a glorious crown, a beautiful wreath for the remnant of his people. He will be a spirit of justice to him who sits in judgment, a source of strength to those who turn back the battle at the gate".* *(Isaiah 28:5-6)*

IT IS FINISHED!

It had been a traumatic few months and at times it seemed that they would never end – or, more accurately, that they would end, but badly! My friend had been diagnosed with ovarian cancer and it was aggressive. As often with this disease, it had been discovered late in its development and now the prognosis was not good. As I received this news I went away to pray and felt God reassure me that my friend would not die but He would hold and surround her with His feathers. I was so encouraged by this promise but curious about the feathers! So I researched references about the mention of feathers in the Bible and looked them up. As I read the passage in Psalm 91 in the NIV, I noticed the use of the word "feathers" and God spoke to me. "Go and buy a card and write this scripture down and look for some feathers". I was not sure where to find feathers but as I walked the dog that morning there were two white feathers lying on the lawn so I eagerly picked them up for my card. I then wrote the Psalm into the card and it read:

> "Surely he will save you
>> from the fowler's snare
>> and from the deadly pestilence.
> **He will cover you with his feathers,**
>> and under his wings you will find refuge;
>> his faithfulness will be your shield and rampart.
> You will not fear the terror of night,
>> nor the arrow that flies by day,
>> nor the pestilence that stalks in the darkness,
>> nor the plague that destroys at midday.
> A thousand may fall at your side,
>> ten thousand at your right hand,
>> but it will not come near you." (Psalm 91:3-7 NIV)

The next day I received a phone call that my friend had been admitted into hospital with a negative reaction to the chemotherapy and had deteriorated. So, collecting my card, I drove down to see her. On arrival at her bedside I noticed she had a pile of other cards all around her and I realized that in all the stress I had forgotten her birthday. As she opened the next card in the pile I was amazed to watch feathers of different colours and sizes fall out onto the bed. My friend began to cry; "God just spoke to me about surrounding me with feathers –

I think I will be OK." Then she opened my card and we cried together. We had a word for breakthrough! From that day forward I knew my friend would live. We still had tough days of fierce battle and the road was not easy but a few years later I received a phone call – my friend had been back to the hospital and she was in permanent remission – it was finished! We had breakthrough and the cancer had not won! My friend was alive and is still alive today, over ten years later.

KEYS OF WORSHIP AND WARFARE

Often we experience a breakthrough and we see a change in a hardened atmosphere; an improvement in the state of someone's health; or the provision of a job after a time of financial hardship; but then the breakthrough seems to stagnate or even sour. The husband who had started coming to church and softened spiritually over the last three months suddenly becomes antagonistic again and refuses to discuss any God issues with you and then becomes even more hostile. Or the pain that had totally disappeared after prayer returns, and you discover you now have a more serious ailment and your health deteriorates again. How do we handle these times of disappointment when the initial advance and change seem to lose momentum and the circumstances drift back to hardship again? How can we secure and maintain our breakthroughs?

We need to understand the spiritual dynamics of breakthrough so that we are able to hold the ground we gain by faith after we have prayed. Maybe the following illustration will help us understand this concept. Often, when we are praying for breakthrough, we have a mental picture of a stone wall representing the obstacle to the breakthrough and our prayers being like a hammer that will finally penetrate and hit through this wall. However, our breakthrough in the spirit is not through an inorganic stone wall, but rather the penetration into a spiritual world that is living and active. In fact, a better illustration would be a knife cutting through skin – as our spiritual breakthrough is more like penetrating a membrane or tearing a veil than smashing through a wall. This then helps us understand our experiences after we have seen a breakthrough. If we are just knocking down a wall with our prayers then once it is down it will stay down as it cannot rebuild itself. But if we are dealing with a membrane or veil, a spiritual atmosphere, if no one continues to stand in the gap to establish this breakthrough, the membrane will just grow back within a quick space of time with scar tissue and the barrier can get even tougher and thicker!

That is why God is calling us to a new strategy of prayer. We see shorter, more intense seasons of warfare prayer that break through the tough atmosphere and then worshipping prayer that stakes the ground of the breakthrough and establishes this new territory for God. All over the world there is a new movement of corporate prayer emerging where people from across the churches in a city take prayer slots around the clock and so we are able to pray without ceasing. We will have times of intense prayer and battle for a situation and then this should be followed by times of prayer with thanksgiving and worship to maintain the breakthrough. We see this model of prayer, the strategic warfare season followed by a maintaining season of intercession and worship, illustrated by the life of Jesus. First we have the picture of Jesus as the living word, a sword of the spirit that pierced the heavens with His life on the cross to win the breakthrough of salvation for every man, woman and child. Then in Hebrews 7:25 we read that Jesus ascended to Heaven and He now ever lives to make intercession for us in the throne room of worship! On the cross Jesus, the living Word, cried out – IT IS FINISHED! This cry of "It is finished" was the final war cry. In the Greek this word is *teleos* which means it has been paid in full, the breakthrough has been accomplished – the task is completed. The cross was an act of spiritual warfare and Jesus won a total victory and triumphed on the cross. But even Jesus now maintains this breakthrough by his continuous prayer and intercession for the salvation of mankind.

DON'T MISS THE SMALL CLOUD

So how do we recognize the moment of breakthrough? Maturity and experience will teach you when to fight and when to wait and worship. There will be seasons of intense prayer and warfare targeted at the particular situation using the specific God given revelation for that problem. Here the "prophetic watchman" anointing is invaluable as it is able to see the issue clearly and then direct and lead the intensive prayer that can give the strategy and help bring the release. But after the intercessors sense there is a shift in the spiritual atmosphere and a breakthrough is appearing, then we need to maintain this breakthrough. We need to keep our arms outstretched through this torn veil and worship and pray. This is where the committed, continuous prayer for an issue, in an atmosphere of thanksgiving and worship, can hold and strengthen the breakthrough. I believe that this is one of the greatest gifts of the emergence of the 24-7 Houses of Prayer, the Burn Rooms and IHOP. All these prayer movements have trained people to pray and worship God and establish an altar of worship in the heart of our neighbourhoods and cities.

In the story of Elijah on Mount Carmel we read in 1 Kings 18 that he prayed seven times for rain and initially nothing shifted. The sky remained shut and the land was still in drought. But then he prayed the seventh time and his servant came back to him with a better report. There was still no rain but this time he could see a cloud as large as a man's fist. This is an improvement. At last we have a crack in the wall – the first signs of breakthrough. I find it interesting that Elijah does not then get back into his birthing position of intense prayer and battle again for the "full breakthrough" but he recognizes this sign in the spirit. As soon as he sees this small cloud he knows that something has shifted and he moves from battle mode to proclamation! He starts to run and announce the breakthrough is coming – the rain is here! It is important that we also discern when our job of intense prayer is finished and recognize the small clouds of breakthrough. Too often we can dismiss the small cloud as we feel it is not significant enough for the breakthrough we need. But frequently the breakthrough starts as a small cloud and then the deluge follows! Do not despise the day of small beginnings! We can believe for hundreds to be saved in our area but then overlook the one person who gets saved in our street and not disciple them well. We must treasure the first fruits of breakthrough and then wait for the rest to follow.

ROOT ISSUES AND INFESTATIONS

When a breakthrough seems stuck sometimes we need to ensure that we are targeting the right issues in order to see the full release. Are we only looking at the fruit or at the root cause? We cannot just deal with the manifesting symptoms but we need to ask God to reveal to us the foundational reasons. We need specific revelation to identify the strongholds so that we can pray and then remove their influence from our lives or nations. Usually the situation or atmosphere has been ongoing and present for some time. So we should not be discouraged if it then takes some time to discern and reform the old ways of thinking and behaviour in the person or the community.

These principles of praying for deliverance and breakthrough work both at the micro scale in individuals' lives and the macro scale of nations and communities. As we begin to work either with the life of a person or the heart of a community we must recognize that there will probably be many layers of infestation and negativity which need freedom. The heart of an individual, or the fabric of our societies, has been defiled and we need specific wisdom about the keys for cleansing this territory. So I began to wonder how we can see breakthrough where there has been layer upon layer of poor choices and the soil of the heart, or the community, has become infested? During this season of seeking God for answers I happened to watch a TV documentary about how to remove flies from the land when it has become infested with insects. The programme described that the reproductive life cycle of flies was 40 days and so if you wanted to clear the land from these flies you had to be meticulous with your sprays and eradication routine for a full 40 days otherwise the flies would just breed from the eggs already waiting in the ground and the life cycle would start again. As I listened to this programme, I began to strategize as God spoke to me about creating 40 day periods of concerted prayer to ambush the strongholds evident in either the community or a person's life. I began to sense that this consistent prayer would penetrate these impenetrable situations with the power of God's Word. God then spoke to me from Matthew 12 where it speaks about Beelzebub, the lord of the flies. Here in this passage we read:

> "But when the Pharisees heard it, they said, 'It is only by Beelzebul, the prince of demons that this man casts out demons.' Knowing their thoughts, he said to them, 'Every kingdom divided against itself is laid waste, and no city or house divided against itself will stand. And if Satan casts out Satan, he is divided against himself. How then will his kingdom stand? And if I cast out demons by Beelzebul, by whom do your sons cast them out? Therefore they will be your judges. But if it is by the Spirit of God that I cast out demons, then the kingdom of God has come upon you. Or how can someone enter a strong man's house and plunder his goods, unless he first binds the strong man? Then indeed he may plunder his house.'" (Matt 12:24-29, ESV)

As I read this scripture again I felt God say: "I have given you a strategy to bind the strong man in his house so that you can plunder his goods. I want you to use the key of 40 days of intentional focussed prayer for this situation and watch the demonic stronghold loose the individual and let them walk free into their inheritance". So for forty days God was asking me to use my spiritual "fly spray" of prayer and eradicate the demonic infestation that had gripped this territory!

BIND THE STRONGMAN

Immediately I knew what my prayer mission should be. I had been talking with a precious couple who were so desperate to have a child. But they could not conceive. They had both had all the relevant tests and there seemed to be no obvious medical issue, but twelve years later they still had no children. As I talked with them I began to look beyond the issue of their barrenness and their medical history and ask further questions. What had their parents' reaction been to their marriage? Had they had negative experiences in any relationships before or during their marriage? As we chatted through their background I began to identify areas of "infestation" that needed freedom. Like most of us, this couple had made some poor choices, but I began to identify other areas which had become strongholds in their lives.

So I shared with them my desire to engage in a 40 day plan to eradicate the enemy and His power from their marriage and life. We took the word of God and I asked them to break bread together regularly in their home as they prayed through the different areas we had identified and then we claimed the release of their child. This couple had never considered some of the words spoken over them by their family, who hated the fact that they were Christians and that they were a mixed marriage. The husband's mother had shouted at him on his wedding day as he left the house: "That b**** will never give you children – you will never be a father." As we uncovered these different situations, the Holy Spirit showed us that we needed to eradicate these word curses and speak life to this couple and bless their marriage. We did this consistently for 40 days. The following month, after the 40 days of our determined prayer, the wife did a pregnancy test and she was pregnant! The curse had been broken. They now have three children and the family is complete!

So let us pray together:

Father, I ask that you will give us a new tenacity and wisdom to pray and see breakthrough. Teach us to pray the prayer of faith and hold fast to the promises you have given us. Help us to be faithful with our long term prayer projects and watch the full harvest mature. Thank you for your strength in the place of prayer. Amen.

 # The Power of Healing Prayer

PRAYING FOR THE SICK

MY HEALING TESTIMONY

In September 1984 my husband, Gordon, along with our 6 month old baby, Nicola, and I arrived in Zimbabwe to work alongside evangelist Reinhard Bonnke and his Christ for all Nations (Cfan) team. I was just twenty-four years old, a young mother and wife, but full of expectation and longing to be used by God to change the nations and see His power released. However, six weeks later I was fighting for my life in a strange land after being involved in a serious road traffic accident.

It was the 27th October 1984 and we had been conducting evangelism meetings in Harare. About 25,000 people had attended the service on this particular evening and we had seen God working in miraculous ways. After a powerful time of prayer in the intercessors' tent we had walked out to see God touch the lame, the blind and the deaf. I was amazed as I watched with my own eyes cripples leaving their inadequate crutches and jumping for joy, as tears rolled down their black shiny faces, shouting, "Jesus has healed me!" Leaving the meeting full of joy, we had just arrived home to a welcome cup of tea when we heard the sound of a car colliding at the traffic lights right outside our house. Soon the gates of our property were being shaken as bystanders shouted for help. We arrived at the scene and discovered that several ministers of President Mugabe's government had been injured in the accident. Immediately we offered our assistance and began administering first aid to the injured. But while I was busy attending to the crushed people inside the car, I was unaware that a seven-ton military truck was speeding down the hill towards these vehicles outside our home. Unable to stop in time, it ploughed into the stationary vehicles. Suddenly I realized what was happening, but it was too late to escape, and so I was crushed between this truck and the cars.

On impact I heard the bones in my legs begin to snap. As I tried to wriggle free and rescue my knees from being crushed by the truck's substantial bumper, I felt the air from my lungs being squeezed as the truck sandwiched me between the cars and its large radiator. Everything from my hips down was crushed in the impact and both my legs were broken in various places. Having stopped to help people injured in the previous car crash, I now found myself in an ambulance being rushed to a hospital in Harare.

Initially it seemed that my severely fractured bones in both legs were the main medical concern. The medical team managed to set my legs in plaster and I was told they would take at least four months to heal during which time I would be confined to a wheelchair. Nicola, my daughter, was just six months old at this time and I wondered how on earth I was going to cope looking after her whilst confined to a wheelchair. But just twelve hours later a serious complication set in and being in a wheelchair became the least of my concerns – I was fighting for my life. Sometimes when a bone is broken, fat tissue can seep into the blood stream, causing a fat embolism. This fat then travels through the blood stream, through the lungs, heart and up into the brain stem causing a life threatening condition. Unfortunately I began to have multiple fat emboli and slipped into a coma. As I fell into this deep coma, the medical staff were increasingly concerned by my lack of response after three days. A scan then revealed that there was extensive brain damage to my brain stem region and they informed Gordon, my husband, that they expected me to die. Word was sent to my family in the UK and my parents came to my bedside. However, they were not ready to say goodbye and they prayed!

This may sound strange, but I am so grateful to God that this terrible accident happened in Zimbabwe and not in England, my home nation. Any English person probably thinks they would be better off in England where there is better medical care. But no, I was happy it happened in Africa where they have better miracle care! In Africa the people are not afraid to passionately get hold of God for hours and pray with a strong authority: "No! Rachel will not die. She will live." And that is exactly what they did. Despite the fact that I had only been in Africa for six short weeks and they hardly knew me, I later discovered that five churches across Harare joined together to storm Heaven night and day until God restored me to health. Twenty-four hours a day there were never less than a thousand people praying for God to do a miracle!

There was also a wonderful girl called Linda who had only been saved three months. She had been working in the Cfan office with me, sorting through decision cards each morning after the altar calls each night. We had chatted about many things over the hours and when she heard the news she rushed to my bedside. Still a young Christian, she did not know her Bible very well but she had great confidence in its power to heal. So she took the Bible and began to read every scripture on healing she could find onto a tape recorder. Once she had recorded her tape she placed it in a walkman, like an ipod, and played these scriptures to me in my coma. She was so committed that she stayed with me twenty four hours a day, sometimes sleeping under my bed so that she could make sure the tape was turned each time one side was completed. During this process the nursing staff came to remove me from my bed for further tests, but as they removed the walkman playing these healing scriptures, the machine monitoring my vital signs suddenly began to beep loudly. In a panic the nurse replaced the walkman, explaining to those assisting to keep that machine near me as I needed this tape to stay alive! Without fully understanding the content of this tape, they had acknowledged the power of the Word. In fact, I was later told that the nursing staff were so impacted by the power of this tape that they had spoken to Gordon and he was able to bring the radiographer to faith in Jesus. There is power in the Word!

As quickly as they were able, my parents arrived in Harare and rushed to my bedside. My Dad, being a man of great faith, stood at the end of my bed and read out the following declaration based on Psalm 118:17-18:

"Rachel, you shall not die but live for the Lord, and you will proclaim that which is within you. For God has chastened you severely but has not given you over to death."

This was a turning point in the fight for my life, because five hours later I woke up totally compos mentis. God had healed me. I still had two broken legs, but He had healed me from the life threatening fat emboli and restored my brain to normal function instantly (although my kids still doubt this sometimes!).

That was the start of my journey of healing, which lasted several years until finally my entire body was fully restored and healed. I spent the ensuing eight months in a wheelchair whilst my bones knitted back together. After that, walking was very painful for a long time. As soon as I was able to stand, Gordon and I made the decision to return to work alongside Reinhard Bonnke, first in Africa and then in the Philippines. It was there, almost four years after my accident, that a couple called Charles and Frances Hunter prayed over me and God touched me powerfully once again.

The Hunters were visiting the Philippines and we were invited to one of their meetings. Charles, whom I didn't know at that time, came over to me and asked me outright, "Excuse me, but can I ask you – is there anything wrong with your body due to a road traffic accident?" A little shocked, I said, "Well, yes, there is." Immediately he said he would like to pray for me and as he did so he reached down and touched my leg. I didn't feel anything at the time, but he then said to me, "Now, do something you could not do before I prayed for you."

Ever since the accident I had not been able to walk anywhere easily without wearing shoes because my right leg was twisted and much shorter than my left. I simply could not get my right heel to touch the ground. Apprehensively I took my left shoe off first, and then my right, and found that for the first time since the accident, both my heels touched the ground. I knew at that moment that God had miraculously lengthened and straightened my right leg. The pain subsided and I have been able to walk perfectly ever since that time.

God had done so much for me, so naturally I had an immense sense of gratitude in my heart. I could not help but be overwhelmed with a sense of, "Wow! People have prayed. I should have died but I am alive. God has healed me!" When you have had a near death experience and know God answered prayer, trust me, you do believe in prayer like never before! So I believe in the prayer for healing!

PRAY FOR THE SICK

My testimony demonstrates the wonderful joy of answered prayer. We do know that God answers our prayer for healing. However, most of us, myself included, have also prayed for people who are sick and they have not been healed. This sense of uncertainty about what will happen often makes us hesitant to offer to pray for healing. We feel a sense of responsibility for their life and anticipate the pain of disappointment if the healing does not happen and so we hold back from offering to pray for the sick. Although this is understandable, it is not right. We are commanded to pray for the sick!

In Mark 16:15-18 we read:

> "And he said to them, 'Go into all the world and proclaim the gospel to the whole creation. And these signs will accompany those who believe: in my name they will cast out demons; they will speak in new tongues; they will pick up serpents with their hands; and if they drink any deadly poison, it will not hurt them; they will lay their hands on the sick, and they will recover.'"

Here in this passage of scripture we are challenged as part of our going and proclaiming the good news about Jesus, to lay our hands on the sick and to expect them to recover. One day, as I was considering my reluctance to pray for the sick because of my fear of failure, God challenged me, "Rachel, has anyone died just because you prayed for them?" "No", I replied, but I got the point! So I continue to lay my hands on the sick people, asking God to bring the recovery. Although not everyone I have prayed for has been healed and some have unfortunately died, NO ONE has ever died *because* I prayed for them. Even though we do not have a guaranteed 100% success rate we still must take the risk and pray for the sick.

CONQUERING THE PAIN OF DISAPPOINTMENT

When we have prayed and the person is still suffering with the illness, or even dies in spite of our prayer, there is a deep sense of disappointment. So how do we process this distress of praying for healing and yet living with the reality that our prayers have not been answered? When hope encounters disappointment our roots of trust and belief are shaken. In fact, this emotion of disappointment can be literally described as the pain of a "missed appointment". We have made an appointment for healing with God and, when it does not happen, we can feel betrayed and confused.

However, the Bible encourages us that those who hope in God will not be disappointed; so how do you reconcile your feelings? In Isaiah we read this scripture:

> "...those who hope in me will not be disappointed." (Isaiah 49:23 NIV)

So even though the circumstances do not make sense, we must not draw back and lose our ability to trust in our relationship with God. Somehow, in the midst of this situation, God is in control! We need to hold fast to our love and trust of God and not allow these disappointments to define our emotions in this moment of pain. The scripture in Romans encourages us as follows:

> "... and this hope does not disappoint us, because God has poured out his love into our hearts by the Holy Spirit, whom he has given us." (Romans 5:2-5 NIV)

Our relationship of hope is based on love and so we must not allow this disappointment to erode our foundational trust in God. Whatever the doubts and fears we have, we need to conquer the disappointments and believe once again that God is for us and will not abandon us. Corrie ten Boom powerfully expresses our need to trust in this statement: "We should never be afraid to trust an unknown future to a known God." So, in the midst of our disappointment, we must ask God to fill us with hope. We need to pray this scripture from Romans: "May the God of hope fill you with all joy and peace as you trust in him, so that you may overflow with hope by the power of the Holy Spirit." (Romans 15:13 NIV) and ask the Holy Spirit to fill us with fresh hope as we make a choice to trust Him, even when everything does not seem to make sense.

WHY DO BAD THINGS HAPPEN TO GOOD PEOPLE?

When you have prayed and believed for healing but the person dies, especially when they are the sweetest person on the earth, it is hard to process and understand. Why are some prayers answered and others not and why do great people have to endure seasons of such harsh difficulty that feel so undeserved? To answer these questions we need to realize that when bad things happen it is not because these good people have now become bad! No – I believe it has more to do with the price of living in a sin-filled society. We need to understand that when we live in an evil society, people are making choices that influence all of our lives, for better or for worse, and since God has given us free choice He chooses not to intervene. Many of these choices made by our communities are not God honouring decisions, they are based on greed and selfishness, and so we as a community pay the price for these choices. Sin has a price – the wages of sin are death – and so we are all affected by these community decisions while we live on earth. For example, our corporate greed or carelessness may affect the way we use nuclear energy, resulting in a similar disaster to Chernobyl. The resulting radioactive dust from such a disaster affects "good" and "bad" people alike and so anyone living in the area could contract cancer. This has nothing to do with the individual's personal holiness but rather it is the effect of living in a less than perfect world. Unjust and unrighteous events can touch our lives too – there will be times of divine protection and escape but there will be other times when we have to face the pressures of everyday twenty-first century life like everyone around us, asking God to give us grace to walk through these times of hardship. Unfortunately, while we are human and living on earth, we will encounter troubles.

DO NOT GET OFFENDED WITH GOD

Difficult times can redefine what the expression, "God is good", truly looks like in everyday life. Gordon often says – "God is good but He is not always nice". In other words, the goodness of God is never in question but there are times when it does not feel so good! When our prayers are not answered as we expect, we need to ensure that we do not get bitter and then lose our relationship with God. God has never promised us a charmed Christian life, with a secure protection plan from all pain. Unfortunately we will suffer hardships and suffering always hurts! But God does promise to walk with us, and hold us through every challenge. Tough circumstances will reveal what is hidden beneath the surface of our heart. We will discover how deep the foundations of trust in our life really are. Many of us have prayed the dangerous prayer – "Oh God make me like you" – but we do not realize that it is during this process of trials and hardship that godly character is developed. We all know this scripture in James that encourages us to enjoy the challenge of hard times:

"Consider it pure joy, my brothers, whenever you face trials of many kinds, because you know that the testing of your faith develops perseverance. Perseverance must finish its work so that you may be mature and complete, not lacking anything." (James 1:2-4 NIV)

So, we need to decide that, when hard times hit our life, we will turn these circumstances into the fertilizer that helps us grow stronger for the next season of our life. Remember, trusting God when life does not make sense is true MATURITY!

KEEP YOUR FAITH AND COURAGE

It takes courage to keep talking to God when life does not make sense. Without this simple child-like faith in God we can shipwreck our lives. In this passage in Hebrews we are encouraged to hold fast to our confidence in God:

"So do not throw away your confidence; it will be richly rewarded. You need to persevere so that when you have done the will of God, you will receive what he has promised. For in just a very little while, 'He who is coming will come and will not delay. But my

> *righteous one will live by faith. And if he shrinks back, I will not be*
> *pleased with him.' But we are not of those who shrink back and are*
> *destroyed, but of those who believe and are saved. Now faith is*
> *being sure of what we hope for and certain of what we do not see."*
> *(Hebrews 10:35-11:1 NIV)*

We need to be people of courage, who continue to believe in the goodness of God even when our circumstances are challenging. Your life may have shifted but He is still the same God who is kind and loving towards you. Do not let your overwhelming circumstances redefine the character of God. Remember He is the same God; He is still in control and intimately involved in your world. Hebrews 13:8 reminds us of this:

> *"Jesus Christ is the same yesterday and today and forever."*

Several years ago now I was due to speak at an evening service when the Pastor phoned to tell me that the church was in shock and would need some gentle handling: their Youth Pastor had just been killed in a traffic accident in Kenya. After praying for the right word, I went to the church and was met by the young widow with her son. I was so amazed by their grace and strength. As I spoke with them they shared how God had spoken to them through a song written by Godfrey Birtill called "You are still God – still God". The young son, only about 7 years old, then looked at me and said – "Even if my Dad dies – God is still God and He will care for us." When everything else changes, God is still God! As I listened to the courage of this bereaved family I was challenged by this truth and their love for Jesus. It is true – whatever has happened – God is still GOD!

REMEMBER, THE END IS NOT THE END UNTIL IT IS THE END!
We tend to feel that when someone dies our prayers have failed and all our efforts were a disaster. This is the end. But a more accurate perspective is that even death is not the end in the family of God.

We have to grasp a bigger picture beyond our loss. Too often we can feel that all our prayer was wasted as the person did not recover. But I believe that our prayer is an investment that cannot be lost. We need to understand that we live in two different time zones when we become a child of God. Heaven runs on *kairos* time, which is the time of eternity. This is circular time without a beginning or an end. But earth runs on *chronos* time, which is the time of natural man. This is linear time – it is the time of yesterday, today and the future. This time has a beginning and an end. God knows the end from the beginning and He is neither surprised nor alarmed by any event. He knows how to work all things together for our good, but can we still love and trust Him? Through the prophet Isaiah God explains to us this principle:

"I make known the end from the beginning, from ancient times, what is still to come. I say: 'My purpose will stand, and I will do all that I please'." (Isaiah 46:10 NIV)

We need to understand that even death cannot destroy the destiny and purpose of God. We see this demonstrated in the life of Jesus, who, even after His death, fulfilled His divine purpose. The end is not the end, only the end of life on earth. Although death will end our dreams, expectations and relationship with the person, which is hard, we also need to realize that, despite our loss, they have not lost; no, in fact, they have gained! As we read these following scriptures we need to understand that there is a reward beyond our prayer being answered on earth:

"All these people were still living by faith when they died. They did not receive the things promised; they only saw them and welcomed them from a distance. And they admitted that they were aliens and strangers on earth." (Hebrews 11:13 NIV)

"These were all commended for their faith, yet none of them received what had been promised. God had planned something

> better for us so that only together with us would they be made
> perfect." (Hebrews 11:39-40 NIV)

We need to understand the eternal dynamic in our natural world;
there are some things that only make sense when we watch from
Heaven's perspective.

ASK INTELLIGENT QUESTIONS

There are times when rather than asking the question, "Why has this
happened?", we should ask the more intelligent question, "Father,
what was your purpose here?" Often the "Why?" question can get us
in trouble as we find ourselves accusing God. But, if we ask God to
reveal His plan in the situation, we can discover the greater objective.

Many years ago, I was a member of a church when we prayed for a
young mum with breast cancer. Unfortunately she died a year later
and I was left confused. As I spent time praying for an answer, I felt
God speak to me about the seeds of faith that had been planted in the
ground as we had prayed as a church. Although we had lost the battle
for the life of this young mum, I felt God say we would see others
healed and these prayers would bring forth a harvest of healing in
the area of cancer. This was NOT the end but the beginning. On the
spiritual landscape we were building a beachhead for breakthrough.
Like Joseph's bones, these seeds of prayer were planted in the land of
our inheritance, but not in the way we thought. Joseph had realized
that he would die before he took hold of his inheritance but he was
still determined to take hold of his promise, whether dead or alive.
We read the account of this story in the passages below:

> "And Joseph made the sons of Israel swear an oath and said, 'God
> will surely come to your aid, and then you must carry my bones up
> from this place'." (Genesis 50:25 NIV)

"Moses took the bones of Joseph with him because Joseph had made the sons of Israel swear an oath. He had said, 'God will surely come to your aid, and then you must carry my bones up with you from this place'." (Exodus 13:19 NIV)

"And Joseph's bones, which the Israelites had brought up from Egypt, were buried at Shechem in the tract of land that Jacob bought for a hundred pieces of silver from the sons of Hamor, the father of Shechem. This became the inheritance of Joseph's descendants." (Joshua 24:32 NIV)

Joseph had physically died but he knew that there would be a day when the breakthrough would come and he was determined to be part of that inheritance. Even when we pray for the sick and we do not see the answer to our prayer we need to continue to watch for the resulting spiritual harvest. So do not let disappointment contain your expectation or limit your prayers. Keep praying for people to be healed and watch as the miracles begin to happen.

JESUS TOUCHED PEOPLE AND HEALED THEM
As Jesus prayed for the sick we can see the power of touching one life at a time. Jesus was able to see the individual in the ocean of pain and focus on their particular need, and change everything. Too often we feel overwhelmed as we see all the needs before us and we allow our sense of inadequacy to dominate rather than the cry of the one sick person. We need to learn to see beyond our emotions to the person and touch their life with Jesus. When we pray for the sick, let us carry the good news of Jesus and stretch out our hands to touch people, ONE after ONE after ONE!

In the following scriptures we notice that praying for the sick was part of the everyday life of Jesus. Everywhere he went he was confronted by the pain of people and he took time to pray with them.

"He touched her hand and the fever left her, and she got up and began to wait on him." (Matthew 8:15 NIV)

"Then he touched their eyes and said, 'According to your faith will it be done to you'." (Matthew 9:29 NIV)

"But Jesus came and touched them. 'Get up', he said. 'Don't be afraid'." (Matthew 17:7 NIV)

"Jesus had compassion on them and touched their eyes. Immediately they received their sight and followed him." (Matthew 20:34 NIV)

"After he took him aside, away from the crowd, Jesus put his fingers into the man's ears. Then he spit and touched the man's tongue." (Matthew 7:33 NIV)

"Then he went up and touched the coffin, and those carrying it stood still. He said, 'Young man, I say to you, get up!'" (Luke 7:14 NIV)

"But Jesus answered, 'No more of this!' And he touched the man's ear and healed him." (Luke 22:51 NIV)

"...and they begged him to let the sick just touch the edge of his cloak, and all who touched him were healed." (Matthew 14:36 NIV)

"And wherever he went – into villages, towns or countryside – they placed the sick in the marketplaces. They begged him to let them touch even the edge of his cloak, and all who touched him were healed." (Mark 6:56 NIV)

Desperate people gathered around Jesus and expected to be healed. Jesus engaged with people from every walk of life and they were healed. Jesus touched the hurting – the dying – the blind – the lame and the tormented. Jesus touched men and women, children and adults. Jesus laid his hands on the sick and brought great healing.

THE POWER OF TOUCHING ONE LIFE!

Once we recognize that prayer is part of our ministry of love to those around us, we can begin to keep the right perspective as we pray for the sick and suffering. Jesus connected with the people in his community and we need to realize that this message of acceptance and love never fails. God has given us a message of HOPE. There is a cry of loneliness in our communities. People carry a sense of hopelessness when they receive bad news about their health, wondering if anyone cares. These are amazing opportunities for us in the church to show that people matter to us. When the Early Church came together and looked at the pressures they were encountering they realized that together they were strong – together they had enough for every need and together they could be a voice of influence!

"All the believers were one in heart and mind. No one claimed that any of his possessions was his own, but they shared everything they had." (Acts 4:32 NIV)

This ability to have all things in common totally undermines the atmosphere of greed and selfishness so often present in our western culture. As we come to pray, care and provide for one another we can reverse the curse of this atmosphere and bring healing to our communities. We can carry this good news of love and start a revolution of change by touching people with prayer and kindness ONE after ONE after ONE.

Just as in the Early Church, we want to see the Church today have a reputation as the place of healing and power. We read in this scripture in Acts that the local community wanted to engage with the Church as they recognized that when they prayed something happened:

"...so that even handkerchiefs and aprons that had touched him were taken to the sick, and their illnesses were cured and the evil spirits left them." (Acts 19:12 NIV)

It is time to let people know that the Church is ready to pray for the sick, the hurting and the desperate in our communities. We need to be ready to pray on the streets.

PRAYING ON THE STREETS

Healing On The Streets, or HOTS, teams have become part of our missional life as the Church these days. The concept of HOTS is a simple, but beautiful, way to reach out to the lost and hurting on the streets of your town or city. It enables you to connect with your community while powerfully expressing God's love in the market place, whatever the weather. You simply invite people to sit on chairs so that you can pray for them. By using prayer and worship you create a place on the streets where Heaven and earth meet; an atmosphere that is spiritually rich and full of the power of the Holy Spirit but with a stillness where people can sense His presence of peace. This gentle ministry works within a loving and compassionate environment. Amongst the hustle and bustle of busy shoppers, passers-by begin to slow and stop, as they notice the banner displaying that prayer for healing is being offered. As conversations start, people soon sit down, and next you are praying for the sick in your community. Suddenly prayer is happening on the streets! The stories and testimonies are exciting and every week someone somewhere is touched as we reach out and pray. Here is a testimony from a prayer team in Canterbury:

"A lady shuffled towards the chairs and sat down and we went over to her. She had an infection in her chest and had had it for a month. Every time she breathed in it really hurt. We prayed for her and after two or three minutes we asked her how she felt and she said she still had the pain. So we asked if she minded if we prayed for her again and reaffirmed that God loved her. We prayed again; they were just very simple prayers – and then we asked, 'how do you feel now?' This time she responded – 'It's gone! The pain has gone!' so we asked, 'Are you sure?' So she breathed in really deeply and confirmed that there was no pain."

So let us overcome every hesitation that we have and begin to pray for the sick with a new confidence. I believe this is a new season and that, as we reach out our hands and touch the sick and the hurting, we will be amazed as we see people healed and changed by God's love.

Prayer:

Father I believe that this is a day for miracles and I ask you to use me to pray for the sick and the hurting. Please help me overcome all my fear, disappointment and anxiety concerning this area of praying for the sick. Help me understand the seasons of loss and unanswered prayer more fully. Restore hope to me and give me a new excitement to pray for healing again. Let me lay my hands on the sick and, Father, will you bring their recovery? Thank you. Amen.

Stake the Ground

CLEANSING THE LAND AND PRAYER WALKING

A raw cry resonated around the prayer room as an older lady prayed with great earnestness repeating this phrase again and again – "No, this cannot happen – No, not on my watch – Not on my watch!" As I listened to her pray, I realized that she was praying for the children in her neighbourhood and was devastated as she watched the brokenness in the marriages and family life all around her. She was ready to stand guard and stake her neighbourhood for God. Here was an intercessor, watching over her territory, recognizing the strategy of the devil but ready to do battle.

This phrase "Not on my watch", and the passion with which she expressed it, continued to resonate in my spirit for several days. I felt challenged by both her willingness to stand in prayer for the children and her sense of responsibility for her community. People and their land are connected – so if we care about people, we need to care about the land too. This is also a very biblical perspective. God expects us to take responsibility for the land in which we live.

GOD'S RELATIONSHIP WITH THE LAND AND HIS PEOPLE

God has a distinct and definite relationship with both the land and the people who live in the land. In Psalm 24 we read:

> "The earth is the LORD's, and everything in it, the world, and all the people who live in it." (Psalm 24:1)

Firstly, God states that the earth is His and then He clearly says "and so are the people". In several places in scripture God talks about His relationship with the people and then His separate, but clear, relationship with the land. One of the most popular scriptures that outlines this thought is found in 2 Chronicles 7:14:

> "if my people, who are called by my name, will humble themselves and pray and seek my face and turn from their wicked ways, then I will hear from Heaven, and I will forgive their sin and will heal their land."

In this passage we notice that the choices we make as individuals to connect with God will both change our lives and affect the land we live in. As we humble ourselves and pray, God promises us that He will forgive us but also heal our land. So the choices we make as we live in our cities and communities will literally affect the well-being of the land.

According to Genesis, God took man and placed him in the Garden of Eden to work it and take care of it (Genesis 2:15). In fact, if you read this phrase translated "work it and take care of it" in the NKJ version, it reads as "dress it and keep it". This is almost the biblical language used when taking care of a wife! A further study of the root meaning of this Hebrew word "shamar" shows it literally means to *work and keep it – guard, protect, attend, keep, preserve, reserve, watch over, steward and present it!* God took man and put him in the garden. Then God gave man a unique relationship and responsibility with this land. Man is required to care for it and then present it to God.

RIGHT PERSON – RIGHT PLACE

Just as God has this vital relationship with both His people and His land so He desires us to have the same. Remember, it is no accident where you are located today. God often moves people throughout scripture so that He has the right person, positioned in the right place, at the right time. Remember Abraham: God called him to move so that he could be given the right land to inherit. We read this account in Genesis where God speaks to Abraham and says:

> "I am the LORD, who brought you out of Ur of the Chaldeans to give you this land **to take possession of it**." (Genesis 15: 7)

This statement, "to take possession of it", is very strong in the original text: it has a literal sense of seizing the land with a firm grip as a mother lioness would seize her cubs in her mouth when she wants to move them! Here God is instructing Abraham to take a firm grip of his territory and hold onto it tenaciously as his inheritance. We need to understand that land with distinct boundaries and borders has been assigned by God to people, and people have been assigned by God to particular portions of land.

OWNING MY TERRITORY

In this passage in Jeremiah we read these sad verses:

> "...the whole land will be laid waste because there is no one who cares." (Jeremiah 12:11)

Here the phrase "no one cares" literally means "no one takes it to their heart"! But God is different as expressed in the book of Deuteronomy:

> "It is a land the Lord your God cares for; the eyes of the Lord your God are continually on it from the beginning of the year to its end." (Deuteronomy 11:12)

Here we read that God is connected to the land and he watches over it with a protective heart year in and year out. God has an interest in the land given to us and the way we will watch over the land appointed to us. We do not live in a geographical area by accident, or just for our convenience, but the Bible says that we have been positioned there for purpose. You may feel that you live in your area just because of your job, or to be near your family, but in the book of Acts we read that God has designated the place where we live:

> "From one man he made every nation of men that they should inhabit the whole earth; and he determined the times set for them and the exact places where they should live." (Acts 17:26)

This scripture teaches us that God is as interested in the place where we live as the time in which we live there. Our geography is important to God and He wants us to take responsibility for this land. It is time to take our cities and streets to heart!

CONNECTED TO MY LAND

If you continue to study this thought about a land and people connection, you will find that there are many references in the Bible concerning this subject. In fact the number of references that connect man with the land, earth or nations are as follows:

- Land – 1462 times
- Earth – 738 times
- Nations – 560 times

As we accept this connection with the land we then realize that we should take responsibility too. We realize that there is work for us to do and we can begin to get intentionally involved as we:

- SPY out the land – do the research and identify the strongholds
- STRATEGIZE – find specific strategies to take back the land and return it to its original purpose

- SACRIFICE – pay a price in time, commitment and resources to see breakthrough
- STAKE – we need to take the word of God and proclaim His goodness over the land.

DO NOT DEFILE THE LAND

So having accepted that land has been assigned to us for a purpose, how do we steward our neighbourhood or city? These days we are made more aware of choosing an environmentally friendly way to live, but do we ever consider the spiritual impact of our lifestyle on the land? Here in Jeremiah God rebukes His people for the way that they have treated their land:

> "I brought you into a fertile land to eat its fruit and rich produce. But you came and defiled my land and made my inheritance detestable." (Jeremiah 2:7-8)

Have you ever considered how we are able to defile land? We know that by our poor choices we can defile our bodies but here we see that sinful choices can defile the land too. The book of Ezekiel carries this thought with 138 references connecting the prophet with his land. Again and again God challenges Ezekiel to stand and speak to the land and repent for the defilement due to the lifestyle choices of the people of the day. One such reference is found in Ezekiel 22:34:

> "Son of man, say to the land, 'You are a land that has not been cleansed or received rain in this day of wrath'."

God explains the need for this cleansing through His prophet Jeremiah, telling them that their immorality and sexual sin has defiled the land:

> "Look up to the barren heights and see. Is there any place where you have not been ravished? By the roadside you sat waiting for lovers, sat like a nomad in the desert. You have defiled the land

> with your prostitution and wickedness. Therefore the showers
> have been withheld, and no spring rains have fallen. Yet you have
> the brazen look of a prostitute; you refuse to blush with shame."
> (Jeremiah 3:2-3, 9)

Israel's immorality was rampant and nobody was ashamed by this fact, so the land was defiled as the people continued to commit adultery and worship idols of stone and wood. We read that this behaviour had an impact on the weather patterns of the nation and God said he would withhold the rain. There would be drought and no spring rain upon which this agricultural nation depended for its healthy economy. Again in Leviticus we read that the continuous sexual sin, immorality and overt sexual perversion in a nation will defile the land and have repercussions.

> "Even the land was defiled; so I punished it for its sin, and the land
> vomited out its inhabitants." (Leviticus 18:25)

If you defile the land, it will vomit you out. If we live in disharmony with our God-given assignment with the land, the land will no longer live in harmony with us. We will experience "the land vomiting us out" and climatic shifts, disasters, droughts or floods will happen around us as the land groans. Just as we speak to the land, so the land "speaks" back to us.

We have seen that both idolatry and sexual sin will defile the land but here in Genesis we also read that when blood is spilt, the land responds. In this passage God talks to Cain about his brother, Abel, and asks him what has happened:

> "The LORD said, 'What have you done? Listen! Your brother's blood
> cries out to me from the ground'." (Genesis 4:10)

God tells Cain that because he has murdered his brother, innocent blood has been shed, and now the land itself cries out. If we consider the land of our nations, I wonder what is the sound speaking out from the ground as a result of all the wars, murder and injustice where so many innocent lives have been lost? There must be a sound of great defilement crying out from the nations. We are called to care for this land and it is time for the Church to fulfil her task.

THE LAND IS CRYING OUT TO THE CHURCH

As we begin to comprehend our role as watchmen working in partnership with the land around us, we gain a different perception when we come to pray in our communities. Suddenly we realize that where we pray, and *what we say*, has power to influence the atmospheres in our neighbourhoods. We begin to appreciate the need for research and a knowledge of history as we begin to uncover the hidden layers of sin that have become a burden on the earth. The Church and creation were designed to cooperate and work together. We read in Luke that when the religious leaders tried to suppress the disciples and stop them praising Jesus, Jesus rebuked them and here we read:

> *"And some of the Pharisees in the crowd said to him, 'Teacher, rebuke your disciples.' He answered, 'I tell you, if these were silent, the very stones would cry out'." (Luke 19:39-40)*

We need to be aware that there are many conversations in the spiritual realms that are not heard with our natural ears and so we can be blissfully ignorant of them. Creation has a voice and it declares its love for God and now the Church needs to join this choir!

In fact, in Romans, we have a wonderful picture of creation all standing on tiptoe waiting and watching for the Church to find its place of authority. I love to read the JB Phillips' translation of this passage:

> *"In my opinion whatever we may have to go through now is less than nothing compared with the magnificent future God has planned for*

> us. The whole creation is on tiptoe to see the wonderful sight of the
> sons of God coming into their own. The world of creation cannot as
> yet see reality, not because it chooses to be blind, but because in
> God's purpose it has been so limited – yet it has been given hope.
> And the hope is that in the end the whole of created life will be
> rescued from the tyranny of change and decay, and have its share
> in that magnificent liberty which can only belong to the children of
> God!" (Romans 8:18-21)

The whole of creation is on tiptoe to see the wonderful sight of the sons of God coming into their own. Creation is waiting for the Church to find its right position and use its authority. Next time you take a walk into your community, imagine every tree and flower, all the creation around you, cheering you on into your destiny and purpose. Creation is speaking with us as we pray!

So we need to engage in prayer, not only for the people, but also for the land where they live. In Isaiah 58 the prophet confronts the religious hypocrisy of those who are praying and fasting. In fact he says that if their prayers are just "nice" words without accompanying actions of love and mercy, their prayers are powerless. He then faces them with their responsibility and says:

> "Is it not to share your food with the hungry and to provide the poor
> wanderer with shelter – when you see the naked, to clothe them,
> and not to turn away from your own flesh and blood?" (Isaiah 58:7)

Here God challenges these people that they need to connect with the people in their nation – "Do not turn away from your own flesh and blood", commands the prophet, and so we too need to turn towards our own people in our nation. Often it is easier to be more missional-minded towards the poor living in nations like Africa and India and forget those here in our own local areas. But, if we want to see breakthrough in our nation, we need to stand with our people living in the deprived areas of our own communities. In Ezekiel 22:30 we read this heart cry of God:

> "I looked for **someone** among them who would build up the wall and stand before me in the gap on behalf of the land so that I would not have to destroy it, but I found no one."

We need to be that "someone" who will stand in our streets on behalf of the land, who will turn our heart towards our broken communities and build up these walls.

STAKE THAT GROUND

There needs to be a new militant cry from our spirits that begins to "own" our territory and mark it for God. Like the cry of the woman in intercession for her community, a shout needs to arise – "Not on my watch – This area belongs to God – We are marking this land for Him!" I own a wonderful chocolate Labrador called Dibley, and we love walking together. One of the rituals of any walk is Dibley's desperate attempt to pee on every tree, lamppost, stone and anything else that defines the boundaries of the properties and paths we journey. Even when his tank has run dry, the ritual continues and he will cock his leg and try to squeeze the last drop out! He is determined to mark his ground and stake his territory! Watching this ritual I felt the Holy Spirit speak to me – "Rachel, you need to mark your turf as you walk and pray – Stake this ground for me!" So what do I mean by "stake the ground"?

"Staking the ground" is a prayer of ownership expressed with authority that defines the boundaries of your mandate; it marks your territory and jurisdiction, with an attitude that says that I am ready to defend this place and declare war on all intruders! But as we stake this ground for God against every plan of the enemy, we also ought to pray for support to reinforce those in our community that need help. If you remember what we discussed in the section on intercession, we come both as the face of the lion and the lamb. We protect the land from every negative spiritual influence but we also decree a blessing in the community.

SET YOUR FOOT

Staking is an intentional and specific act both in the natural and the spiritual realm. When Joshua is commanded to go and take hold of his inheritance, God gives him specific instructions about exactly which areas he is called to possess. We read this account here:

> "Now then, you and all these people, get ready to cross the Jordan River into the land I am about to give to them – to the Israelites. I will give you every place where you set your foot, as I promised Moses. Your territory will extend from the desert to Lebanon, and from the great river, the Euphrates – all the Hittite country – to the Mediterranean Sea in the west. No one will be able to stand against you all the days of your life. As I was with Moses, so I will be with you; I will never leave you nor forsake you." (Joshua 1:2-5)

Joshua is given this specific land but still told to go and physically "take it" by placing his foot on the territory. God promises that He will give him all the places where he SETS HIS FOOT.

In this verse, "*I will give you every place where you **set your foot***", the phrase "set your foot" has a strong image associated with it. In the days of Joshua, when the warriors came to battle, they would carry their long bows and when the command was given, "set your foot", the archers prepared to fire by placing their foot on the base of the bow, and then firing their arrows. To "set your foot" was a warfare term. So when we "set our feet" in our community, this is more than a casual wandering through the neighbourhood; there needs to be a spiritual engagement that is declaring: "this belongs to us!" There needs to be a definite objective both practically and spiritually that is given to us by God. Staking doesn't happen by accident or by default. God promises to give us this ground as we walk out with His word into our communities. Staking has to do with walking with these God-given promises and claiming back our territory into its rightful Kingdom purpose.

PRACTICAL PLANNING FOR YOUR PRAYER WALK

There are three definite stages in the planning process that will help you engage as you go prayer walking. Basically they are: what you need to prepare before you go, what you should do while you are walking, and what you need to do once you return.

1. BEFORE YOU GO

Decide the purpose and location

Before deciding to go and prayer walk, ask God to show you the purpose of your prayer walking. I know God called me to go and walk the streets of London so that I would become familiar with the city and its various needs. Once you know why you are prayer walking, ask God to show you the dimensions of the geographical assignment He has given you. Maybe you already have a regular route that you walk to work and He wants you to claim this walk as prayer walking time, or perhaps you need to get a map out and ask God to show you which are the areas of your geography that He has assigned to you to watch over. In Isaiah 62:6 it states that "God has assigned watchmen on the walls" to watch over the city. I believe that God has given us specific duties on behalf of our communities. So let God assign you as a watchman for your geography. Listen to Him and then take your responsibility and go out on spiritual patrol duty.

Decide on the strategy and method

Before you leave to prayer walk, it is good to ask God to give you a strategy while you pray. Take time to look at specific prophecies and promises given for the area. Read your Bible and ask God to give you particular verses that declare the heart of God for your area and speak them out as you walk. For example, if you know God has asked you to go and pray specifically about the violence in your neighbourhood, you could prepare scriptures to take with you. Remember the words that you speak are like beams of light penetrating the dark places. So, when you are looking for the right verses to take with you, identify the spiritual atmosphere and then find the promises of God which speak the opposite atmosphere/spirit and speak out these words over the area. If you are praying for salvation to come to your area, then you could prepare some scriptures concerning salvation and pray them over the houses as you walk by. You can use scripture both as an instrument of blessing and as a spiritual weapon. Psalm 149:6-9 states:

> *"May the praise of God be in their mouths and a double-edged sword in their hands, to inflict vengeance on the nations and punishment on the peoples, to bind their kings with fetters, their nobles with shackles of iron, to carry out the sentence written against them. This is the glory of all his saints."*

God's Word is a double-edged sword that can do serious damage to the enemy's territory. As a result of declaring it over the land we are affecting the spiritual atmosphere of the community around us.

Hebrews 4:12-13 also speaks of the dynamic, living power of the Word:

> *"For the word of God is living and active. Sharper than any double-edged sword, it penetrates even to dividing soul and spirit, joints and marrow; it judges the thoughts and attitudes of the heart. Nothing in all creation is hidden from God's sight. Everything is uncovered and laid bare before the eyes of him to whom we must give account."*

The word "active" means that it is operative, powerful, and effective. So when we pray using scripture we can speak with confidence knowing that we are praying in agreement with God's will. As we declare this revealed Word of God over the community we hit the right target every time.

Prepare items you need to take with you

As you prepare your heart, you may find that God gives you specific practical actions that He wants you to perform as you walk through the community. Be open to hear and then prepare the necessary items. You may want to break bread and share communion within your group on one of the high places near your town and so will need to take the bread and wine. You may want to mark maps with observations as you walk. You may feel that you want to put stakes into the ground that carry the promises of God. All these items will need to be prepared and taken with you on your walk. So be prepared!

Prepare information and pray for discernment

As we prepare to walk into the community, we need to be aware that we must train both our spiritual and natural eyes and ears to "see" and "hear" what both God and the land are saying. Prepare some information before your walk so that you have a general grasp of the geography, statistics of the areas and outline history. Take time to research the meaning of significant place names in the area and discover if the city has a motto or special dates or customs. Then with this knowledge ask God to increase your sensitivity to discern the spiritual atmospheres. Expect God to reveal to you "hidden" information about your area. Take time to listen to God in the private place so that in the public place you will hear His voice more easily. Remember the Holy Spirit can be like a metal detector: when you get near a problem an alarm sets off in your spirit and you need to learn to listen to this warning sound and know what it means.

2. WHILE ON THE MOVE

Now you are out on the streets prayer walking, what should you do and how do you pray and respond?

Walk out knowing God is with you

Remember you are on Kingdom business, responding to Heaven's call and so, as you walk out, go as His ambassador carrying your diplomatic status in your community. So walk, confident that God is with you, and that He has given you authority over the land where you place your feet. Joshua 1:9 says:

> *"Have I not commanded you? Be strong and courageous. Do not be terrified; do not be discouraged, for the LORD your God will be with you wherever you go."*

As you walk in faith, remember that God will protect and help you. So do not let fear or intimidation confuse your mind, but walk knowing God is with you and will anoint you to pray effectively.

Declare the "God" ideas

As you walk in your area, ask God to remind you of the relevant research that you have done and declare the heavenly purpose connected to the name or mottos you have found. For many years I lived near Hemel Hempstead, in Hertfordshire. I discovered that this name was derived from the German meaning Heavenly Homesteads. The statistics show that Hemel Hempstead has anything but heavenly homes, so when we prayer walked this area, we declared the redemptive purpose of God on this community and prayed that the homes would reflect Heaven! Ask the Holy Spirit to reveal the redemptive purpose of your area to you – in other words, declare over the land what it should be like if fully yielded to God's agenda.

Often you can use the scriptures or promises you know God has given you in your times of preparation and speak these out. I know I often use this scripture in Britain as I feel this is a promise for our nation:

"Arise, shine, for your light has come, and the glory of the LORD rises upon you." (Isaiah 60:1)

I speak it over the community, praying that it is time to arise and carry our Christian heritage once again.

Keep connected to Jesus

As you are prayer walking, remember to stay connected to Jesus and surround yourself with an attitude of worship and praise. Do not be afraid to sing to yourself and declare His praises in the streets – you do not have to sing at the top of your voice! It is this proclamation of praise that is like a sharp sword, which helps pierce through the spiritual darkness. Pray and declare the scriptures you have prepared beforehand. It is good to have written them down so they are accessible, unless you have memorized them.

Speak blessing to the community

Keep a happy face as you walk, smile and be ready to talk to someone if they stop you. Don't look intense and religious! As people pass you, pray a prayer of blessing for them. Try to pray more than "God bless them" – pray for peace, for joy etc. As you watch them approach you, ask God to show you their needs. If He gives you a specific word of blessing ask God for an opportunity to share it. Bless the people of your community with the love of Jesus as you pass them in the street. I would recommend that you do most of this silently but do speak to those God shows you and give them a word of life.

Ask for angelic protection for your community

In Hebrews we read this verse:

"Are not all angels ministering spirits sent to serve those who will inherit salvation?" (Hebrews 1:14)

I believe that as people who have been saved, we can ask God to send angels to assist us in our community work. I believe that the natural and the spiritual realms need to work in alignment and that God loves deploying angels to help us do our Kingdom work. We need the angelic security guards on duty on our streets!

Pray for the economic climate of your area

As you walk and pray, notice any significant business institutions and industries in your area. Make a note of these on your map. Be aware of the economic state of the industrial facilities and shopping centres. Take note of the number of "for sale" boards and properties that are empty or derelict. Remember, if people lose their work then the whole local economy suffers. Speak the blessing of God over the finance and industry in your locality. Some friends of mine in Utica, New York State, really prayed for their area after three major companies closed. They began to call forth jobs into the area and now major new clients are moving their business there, providing the jobs that were lost. The city is coming out of poverty! Pray for the residential homes with "FOR SALE" signs and ask for quick and excellent sales and good tenants in the new "TO LET" properties.

Take time to stop and ask for revelation

As you walk the streets, take time to pause and just watch. Remember every face is cherished, and every door holds a story. Watch the way people connect; is there an atmosphere of loneliness? Ask the Holy Spirit to give you words of knowledge that will help you pray intelligently for the area in future.

Bless the churches

As you walk, bless the churches as you see them. Read their notice boards and discover a little of their interests. Find the Minister's name and pray for him, and remember to thank God for the diversity of the Christian expression you have in your area. Ask God to show you how to pray for each church and pray that they will grow. Also take a note of the other religious institutions in your area.

Be ready for divine appointments

One day I went prayer walking through Watford town centre. I had my plans but as I neared the top of the High Street I met a work colleague from five years ago. Immediately she touched my arm and said, "Rachel, I cannot believe this! I was just thinking about you!" She then shared that her mum was ill and she was on her way to the hospital but she was so frightened her mum would die. God gave me the opportunity to pray with her, reconnect my friendship for a season, and then help her through her time of loss. So be ready for those unusual meetings and be prepared to change all your well-intentioned plans!

3. AFTER THE WALK

Pause for a moment and give thanks!

Take a moment just to reflect on the goodness of God. Often you feel so full of inspiration and information after a time of prayer walking that you just need to stop, reflect and thank God. Take a moment to go over the walk in your mind and just thank God for all the little details that He showed you. Even if you cannot see any immediate tangible effects from your walk, trust and know that your prayers will have a harvest.

Protect the seed you have sown

Every prayer that you have prayed is like a seed of promise lying on the ground of your community. Pray that God would protect these "seeds" of prayer that you have sown. Often we do not see the answers immediately, but do watch the local newspapers and wait to see what will happen. You may see the headlines of a major drug haul on an estate and realize that this was where you had just been praying and declaring "let light come into the darkness"! This is exactly what happened to some of my friends after they had been prayer walking in Liverpool, UK.

167

Write a report for your journal

Remember to write down your impressions, scriptures and any prophetic senses that you had as you prayed and keep a note of any information that you collected. Also, as you were prayer walking you may have noted areas that you wanted to research further – put these comments in your action box. Remember to update your map with any information that you have collected. You may find that you need to prayer walk an area more than once. If you have been prayer walking as part of a group then compare your notes with others. If you discover that the different groups have had similar themes and scriptures then take note of these as God is highlighting these issues as being important.

Enjoy the glow of mission accomplished

Sit and just enjoy the presence of God, put your feet up, enjoy some worship music with a big mug of good coffee and let God bless you. Don't just rush into your next list of tasks but take a few minutes to sense the gratitude of God as He blesses you for your obedience. Well done – you have done a good job!

I believe that this is a new season for leaving our footprints on the streets of our villages, towns and nations. God spoke to me about planting new seeds of prayer that will leave a legacy. As God spoke this phrase to me, I realized I was literally crunching on acorns that had dropped onto the ground from a huge oak tree above me. Acorns leave a legacy for hundreds of years so treasure the prayer you have pressed into your streets.

WATCHMEN ON THE WALLS

As you make time to walk and stake the land spiritually with those promises of God, God then gives you a prophetic mandate for that area. As we speak to God, we find He begins to reveal to us strategy about this neighbourhood, city or nation. Recently when I was travelling to Norway I began to hear this refrain "Oh land – Oh land – Oh land!" turning in my spirit as I prayed. I knew that God was calling Norway with great tenderness but I knew that it was also calling Norway into her destiny. This was a gentle cry from the heart of God – "Oh Norway take your place"! God is calling out to many of us to be His watchmen over the nations in this hour. So will you take time and begin to watch over some territory for the kingdom of God?

In these passages from Ezekiel, the Bible describes our responsibility as watchmen in the nation. Here God instructs His prophet that, as His watchman, he needs to be ready to speak God's words of correction and warning. We can read these scriptures as follows:

"Son of man, I have made you a watchman for the house of Israel; so hear the word I speak and give them warning from me." (Ezekiel 3:17)

Then, later in the book, we read this passage:

"But if the watchman sees the sword coming and does not blow the trumpet to warn the people and the sword comes and takes the life of one of them, that man will be taken away because of his sin, but I will hold the watchman accountable for his blood. Son of man, I have made you a watchman for the house of Israel; so hear the word I speak and give them warning from me." (Ezekiel 33:6-7)

God has called us to be His royal priesthood and take responsibility in His Kingdom. We have been given the Great Commission and commanded to go into the whole world and take the message of Good News with us. But, as we go, we must be aware of which spiritual powers are controlling and influencing the lives around us. We are called to be watchmen, who should be aware of the trends and evil influences that dominate the people and government institutions around us. God instructs His prophet that he should give the people direction and, if necessary, a warning about the events that are happening. In the same way, the Church has a responsibility to speak out. We should be crying "Not on my watch!" There should be a militant cry from the Church, raising an alarm or warning, and providing communities with spiritual protection. This is the time to WATCH and then PRAY!

WATCH AND PRAY

So how do we watch and pray? I learnt this lesson working with Reinhard Bonnke at an evangelistic campaign in Blantyre, Malawi. I had been asked to work in the special ministry area where we prayed with many demon-possessed people who were gripped with witchcraft powers. One particular evening we had foreign visitors come to the service and one of these pastors decided to join us in the deliverance area. My African co-worker looked concerned as this rather small, thin white man joined us and began to pray with his eyes tightly shut in a very loud voice. "Mama", my co-worker said to me, "tell your pastor he needs to watch and pray. He must watch and pray!" He had hardly finished expressing his concern when a very large woman, probably weighing over 350lbs, screamed loudly and jumped on top of this pastor whose eyes were still tightly shut. This poor man just disappeared under her weight and the power of her demonic screaming. As I watched this scenario with horror, wondering what I should do next, I could still hear my co-worker exclaiming – "But remember you must watch and pray – please watch and pray!"

So what do we mean by WATCH and PRAY? To watch in the spirit means to be spiritually alert and attuned. You are watching the situation both with your natural intuition and wisdom and with your spiritual discernment. You need to read the signs, body language and attitudes around you. As you watch you ask God to show you His perspective and look at the situation from different world views asking for motivations and intentions to be revealed. You are on a mission with God, and like a community police officer, you watch in the spirit knowing that you have an authority to challenge illegal behaviour. So what areas are we instructed to watch and pray over?

Watch over yourself

As we come to pray, we need to ensure that we watch over our own lives first. We need to pray and ask for God's protection from all deception and ensure that we are making good choices before we watch over others and warn them. Paul encourages Timothy, his apprentice in the Lord:

> "Watch your life and doctrine closely. Persevere in them, because if you do, you will save both yourself and your hearers." (1 Timothy 4:16)

I believe this is always a good place to start. We need to realize that we are not always the best judge of our own personal integrity. Remember this scripture in Samuel:

> "For the Lord sees not as man sees: man looks on the outward appearance, but the Lord looks on the heart." (1 Samuel 16:7)

Our assessment of our motivations and heart responses are not always accurate. So it is important to keep a teachable attitude and transparent relationships with a few trusted friends and ask them to help you watch over your life. Also actively pray and give God permission to challenge and search your heart. Echo this cry from the Psalms:

> "Search me, God, and know my heart; test me and know my anxious thoughts. See if there is any offensive way in me, and lead me in the way everlasting." (Psalm 139:23-24)

Before you try to change the world, take time to listen to the Shepherd of your life and let Him lead you in the right paths.

Watch over the homes

As Nehemiah considers the broken down walls and suffering in his community, he calls his leaders together to stand with him to protect the homes. Here we read:

> "Therefore I stationed some of the people in the lower places behind the wall, and on the higher places, I even set the people after their families with their swords, their spears, and their bows. After I looked things over, I stood up and said to the nobles, the officials and the rest of the people, 'Don't be afraid of them. Remember the Lord, who is great and awesome, and fight for your brothers, your sons and your daughters, your wives and your homes.'" (Nehemiah 4:13-14)

In this season I believe that God is asking us to now stand and watch over our households too.

Today we meet wounded people everywhere, many of whom have been traumatised by a dysfunctional family life. Recent information released concerning the welfare of the family, marriage and home life styles in the western world makes sad reading. The facts show that people are full of anxiety about their future, mistrust concerning their marriage, and experience violence in their homes. The statistics and figures concerning mental health issues, even amongst children in the UK and other nations, also make worrying reading. When you read these figures and imagine the lives affected by these traumas, we realize that we need to watch and pray. We can identify with the prophet Micah who wrote this description of life in his day:

> "What misery is mine! I am like one who gathers summer fruit at the gleaning of the vineyard; there is no cluster of grapes to eat, none of the early figs that I crave. The faithful have been swept from the land; not one upright person remains. Everyone lies in wait to shed blood; they hunt each other with nets. Both hands

are skilled in doing evil; the ruler demands gifts, the judge accepts bribes, the powerful dictate what they desire – they all conspire together. The best of them is like a brier, the most upright worse than a thorn hedge. The day God visits you has come, the day your watchmen sound the alarm. Now is the time of your confusion. Do not trust a neighbour; put no confidence in a friend. Even with the woman who lies in your embrace guard the words of your lips. For a son dishonours his father, a daughter rises up against her mother, a daughter-in-law against her mother-in-law – a man's enemies are the members of his own household." (Micah 7:1-6)

Here is an accurate account of life when the walls of society and community have been broken down. What is encouraging is that it is not a surprise to God and He has a solution for this crisis. Again and again through the years of history we read the accounts of family breakdown followed by the redemption of God as He brings His answer. So here we are again and we need to watch and pray!

Watch for the prodigals

I believe we also need to watch for the prodigals to return to God. Just like the Father in the story of the Prodigal Son, we need to be standing and watching for the return of those who have walked away from church and are now deciding to come back home. We need to create a safe environment where the lost can be welcomed home and find Jesus again. This is a returning season for many. So let us watch and pray for them using this powerful promise:

"And he will go on before the Lord, in the spirit and power of Elijah, to turn the hearts of the fathers to their children and the disobedient to the wisdom of the righteous – to make ready a people prepared for the Lord." (Luke 1:17)

We need to be encouraged because it is often when we least expect a response that we witness the "suddenly" of God. You may feel that

173

your prodigal will never come home so let this story encourage you. We were ministering in a church in California and asked people who were discouraged as a result of praying for an issue where they had seen no result to come forward. We found ourselves praying with a middle-aged man who had not seen his parents for over two years. His parents had refused to see him because of his faith and all contact had been cut. So we prayed and asked God to do a miracle as it was Father's Day that weekend. Imagine our surprise when we returned to the church for the Saturday evening service, only to be greeted by this man smiling from ear to ear. "You'll never guess what happened", he said, "my phone rang this afternoon and it was my Dad and they have agreed to come and have lunch with me tomorrow! I am so excited as I have been waiting years – now suddenly we are talking!" We have just returned to this same church again this year and one of the first people to greet me was this man who told me that his parents are still talking to him and he is even allowed to talk about God now.

Watch over the next generation

This is the area that I find grips many intercessors. As we come and stand in the gap for the next generation, God touches our heart and often there is a mixture of many tears and strong cries for freedom. One of my favourite scriptures that I love to use when praying for the children is this one in Lamentations:

> "Arise, cry out in the night, at the beginning of the night watches! Pour out your heart like water before the presence of the Lord! Lift your hands to him for the lives of your children, who faint for hunger at the head of every street." (Lamentations 2:19)

I believe that, as we watch over the lives of the next generation in prayer, we can shift the trends. There is a new breed of dedicated young people ready to fight for justice and pray through the night. All over the nation, the youth are flocking to prayer rooms to be part of many radical prayer initiatives. Although the enemy has done so much to plunder this generation, God still has His remnant and they are ready to stand and speak out. We need to pray for courage and wisdom to be upon them as they influence and get ready to lead the next movement of God in the nation. So lift up your hands for the children and youth and remember to watch and pray for this incredible generation.

Watch over the nation

All through this chapter we have underlined the necessity to take responsibility for our nation as well as for the people. Here another prophet, Joel, emphasizes this point again:

> *"Blow the trumpet in Zion, declare a holy fast, call a sacred assembly. Gather the people, consecrate the assembly, bring together the elders, gather the children, those nursing at the breast. Let the bridegroom leave his room and the bride her chamber. Let the priests, who minister before the Lord, weep between the portico and the altar. Let them say, 'Spare your people, Lord. Do not make your inheritance an object of scorn, a byword among the nations. Why should they say among the peoples, 'Where is their God?'"*
> *(Joel 2:15-17)*

If you read any history you will find that in moments of national crisis there have been several occasions when the presiding government would call a day of national prayer. The last official national day of prayer in the UK was called by Sir Winston Churchill during the Second World War. Unfortunately, although there are still many crises in the nations, our governments no longer sound the alarm and call the people to gather and pray! But I believe that we, the Church, still need to gather and pray at certain times. It has been so thrilling to watch prayer movements and churches begin to partner together in the UK, Europe and other nations to hire stadiums and large facilities for the purpose of prayer.

We need to possess the nation, take hold of it and stake this ground! We can often feel we are too small and insignificant to have any influence in a nation. What can we do? Let me share with you this picture. I was praying in London and as I looked at the vast city I wondered what difference my "little" prayer could make, and then God showed me an illustration. Just near to where I was walking were some men standing around a telephone pole. As I approached, I realized that they had just replaced this pole as the old, rotten one lay on the ground near to where they were working and now they were attaching the cables to this new pole. They had "staked" the ground with this new pole and now they were restoring the communication lines. God then spoke to me and said – "Rachel, I am not asking you to touch every piece of land, just this place I have given you and, as you stake this ground, you will open the communication lines across the nation and, as each one positions their pole, the nation can be connected in this network". Just as the new telephone poles need to be repositioned to carry the cables, so we need to find our place and stake this piece of territory in prayer so that we can connect together and cover the nation with God's supernatural communication network!

It is easy to see what is decaying and rotten when we watch over the lives of people and their communities but God is asking us to raise a new standard. He is giving us the privilege of decreeing a new season of breakthrough. As we engage in prayer, cry out for the healing of our land and watch over His Word, we will see marriages restored, churches revived and nations transformed.

Prayer:

Father we ask that you would take our lives and use them to transform our communities and nations with your love. We believe that this is a time for shift and change. Please teach us to pray and walk in our communities and set our feet where you are positioning us. Open our eyes and help us watch and pray for our homes, children and nation. Let the raw cry of "Not on my watch" resound from our hearts as we stand on behalf of the broken. Thank you for your authority and power upon our lives. Amen.

 Capital Cities

PRAYING FOR GOVERNMENTS, JUSTICE AND RIGHTEOUSNESS

As you begin to watch over the nations you will also begin to notice that it is hard to separate the nation from the influence of its capital and major cities. Capitals with their prominent larger cities carry significant authority which then shapes the culture of a nation. If you think of Japan, you immediately think of Tokyo; if you mention England, you see London; and it is hard to talk about the United States without considering the influence of New York, Los Angeles, San Francisco, Washington DC and the many other major cities of America. Capitals and larger cities carry significance and affect the spiritual atmosphere of the nation because of their vast global connections, opportunities and power. So as we begin to open our hearts to the nations we also find God challenges our heart concerning cities too.

SURPRISED BY MOLDOVA

At Heartcry for Change God supernaturally opened doors for us to partner with some wonderful people in Moldova. As we began to support them in their work, I felt it was necessary for us to go and literally pray in the land in order to sense the atmosphere of this nation. At this time I did not know the culture or understand any of the issues facing this nation. We soon discovered that Moldova has been controlled by many ungodly regimes and influences that had shaped its culture. So right at the beginning of our involvement there we took time to let Jesus touch our hearts with His love for this nation. A prayer team, led by Helen Azer, went to pray in Chisinau and so began our love journey with this precious nation. Here is the story of their adventure:

> In April 2014 a team of us visited Chisinau, the capital city of Moldova. We had planned this prayer assignment six months earlier, not knowing that our timing would be so perfect. Only weeks previously, the Ukrainian Crimea region had been invaded by Russian troops and the whole region was inflamed with old divisions. Moldova is a tiny nation sandwiched between Romania and the Ukraine with a high proportion of Russian speakers. The day before we arrived to pray, the EU had granted Moldovans visa free access into Europe and the streets of the capital were decked out with European flags. It felt like battle lines were being drawn between those who wanted to move into a new era with integration into the European Union and those who longed to go back to the "good old days" and strengthen their ties with Russia.

> As we stepped out of our hotel, we asked God what we should decree and wondered what our mandate should be at such a critical time. Then one of our team spotted a car with this number plate "CRY 555". As we saw this, we realized God was speaking to us: "Cry Grace, Grace, Grace!" (Biblically 5 often represents the concept of grace). Of all the sounds we could release over this capital city, we felt God say that He wanted us to speak grace to the city.

> Fast forward three days to our final day. We had covered a huge amount of ground, literally and spiritually! Now, as we

were about to leave, we asked God to give us a sign of what He was doing in this precious nation. We decided to go and stand in front of the national parliament building and declare the promises of God for the nation. As we did this, we noticed that there was a lot of activity around the building: men were busily raking up the soil and then, as we watched, they began to lay down new turf. Immediately we felt the Holy Spirit say to us, "I am doing a new thing in this nation. This is a new day. You are standing on new ground (turf!)". We were then reminded of the scripture from Isaiah 35 which promises that the wilderness will blossom.

As we asked God to give us a love for this nation, He told us to go and pray in the capital. Here God touched our hearts, gave us prophetic insight and allowed us to see both the natural government and our spiritual authority working together for the sake of a nation. So now maybe you should ask yourself this question – do you take responsibility and pray for your nation and capital city, or do you just pray for people?

THE CAPITAL CITY CHALLENGE

Jesus wept. When Jesus saw His capital city He wept. There was something drawn out of the depths of His being as He stood and looked at this capital city, Jerusalem, and He found Himself moved to intercession. What is your response when you think about the capital city of your nation? Do you weep and pray? Too often we approach our cities with a negative attitude. Often I hear Christians complain when they speak about their cities. They demonize them as places of evil, chaos, sexual sin, difficult parking, expensive bills and other challenges. For many different reasons people tend to reject the capital city of their nation. I remember sharing about our responsibility to pray for London in the north of England and immediately sensed a hostile reaction. After the session a woman approached me: "I hate

London", she declared angrily, "It robbed me of my daughter! She went to university there and I lost her. She has never been the same since. I will NEVER bless London!" As she left, not wanting to engage in any discussion, I realized with sadness that if we will not weep for our city and pray against the enemy activity, it will rob us of our next generation. If we let our natural prejudices prevent us from praying for these huge power centres, we will never change our nations. If we curse rather than bless, we abdicate our authority in the place of prayer and the land will stay defiled.

This is why Jesus wept as we read in Luke 19:

> "But as he came closer to Jerusalem and saw the city ahead, he began to weep. 'How I wish today that you of all people would understand the way to peace. But now it is too late, and peace is hidden from your eyes. Before long your enemies will build ramparts against your walls and encircle you and close in on you from every side. They will crush you into the ground, and your children with you. Your enemies will not leave a single stone in place, because you did not recognize it when God visited you.'" (Luke 19:41-44)

There is a battle for these national cities of significance and the Church must take its place to establish a true voice of righteousness. This is the ground where both natural and spiritual authority collide. This is a geographical place of alignments where we literally need to see God's order and the national government come into agreement. Jesus wept as He realized Jerusalem had missed God's time of opportunity. As the Church, we need to be advocates for His Kingdom and influence these gates of power to reflect the glory of God. As Christians, I believe we have a huge responsibility to stake this ground of our cities for Jesus. Capital cities are special and they need our tears!

LOVE AFFAIRS WITH CAPITAL CITIES

So how can we love and identify with these huge sprawling cities, with chaotic traffic, exorbitant prices and unsafe environments? Each of us needs to go on a journey with the Holy Spirit and let Him teach you to love the people and the streets. How can we love a nation or a huge city of millions? You need to love it one face at a time. As you walk down the street let the pain of loneliness or anxiety, written on the face rushing by, speak to you and pray for the city and its people from your heart.

My love affair with London started in 1992. This was a God designated assignment where He "infected" my heart with a supernatural connection with London. At the time I did not feel particularly British, since I grew up in India until I was 16 years old, served as a missionary with Gordon, my husband, in Africa and had not lived in the UK for any continuous length of time. I was now 32 years old and unexpectedly God captured my heart for this great city. One morning I woke up and He spoke to me: "Rachel, let me take you by the hand and walk you through the streets of London!" At that time I was so uninformed about my nation I did not even realize that this was the famous Londoners' song! So I arranged for a young man with a passion for London and a heart of prayer to show me his city. This was not just a simple tourist trip looking at the sights, but a look beyond the historic facades to listen to the raw cry of the city of London. We took three days and walked the streets. We stopped in the poor areas where the homeless, prostitutes and alcoholics congregated. We walked the corridors of power through the courts of justice, five star hotels and palaces of the rich and famous. We looked at plaques, visited churches and traced the steps of past revivals and people of God who had preached in these streets. When we had finished walking my heart was burning and breaking all at the same time. God had impregnated me with a passionate love and cry for my city. But I also heard the groaning of the streets of London that day and knew I would never be the same.

Like Nehemiah there is a moment when the city that you are so familiar with at one level suddenly begins to grip your heart. Nehemiah had just read a report about the state of his city and this time the statistics were more than numbers, they penetrated his soul and he felt their effect:

> "When I heard these things, I sat down and wept. For some days I mourned and fasted and prayed before the God of Heaven." (Nehemiah 1:4)

For years you are able to just go to work and only engage on the surface with the city life around you, but one day God shows you the city and you see it at a whole different level. Here we read that Nehemiah had obtained information and this information had opened up his heart of intercession:

> "Those who survived the exile and are back in the province are in great trouble and disgrace. The wall of Jerusalem is broken down, and its gates have been burned with fire." (Nehemiah 1:3)

The report Nehemiah heard was like what you could read today about many of our modern cities. Most of the city is just a huge mass of busy lives trying to raise their families under considerable pressure. Cities are full of people wanting to pursue the right morals, parents trying to educate their children, fathers trying to earn enough money to pay the bills as life rushes past. However, in the midst of this swirling city are the stories that break your heart. You read about a ninety-year-old woman who is mugged and robbed by a gang for just £10, young people dying of drug abuse, a mother who commits suicide at the train station; and you know the walls of the city are broken down.

The report Nehemiah read said that the gates of the city had been burned by fire. Gates represent the seats of government and authority. Our cities have lost their grace and respect for authority. We have some people in government who abuse their power and others who use control and manipulation. However, we are called to rebuild these gates and change the culture of large cities. We have got to let the reports about the pain in our cities affect us. Let the Holy Spirit irritate you with this information; do not get bitter and react against the government institutions but let your heart weep and then respond to the call and bring change. Can you hear your city calling?

CAPTIVATED BY CAPITALS

God is gripping a new breed of people, like Nehemiah and Daniel, who will stand with strong, informed hearts and penetrate the cities with a new code of Godly standards. We do have an urban prayer movement of radical young people who want to change the statistics of our cities and make them havens of peace. They have seen the pain and suffering and they are ready to explore and be part of the cry for justice. Here is the journey of one such radical student, Helen Azer:

> My journey with capital cities started as a 19-year-old student on my year abroad as part of my university degree course. I was in Germany as an English language teaching assistant and, during the half-term break, took the opportunity to travel to Berlin and spend a few days exploring the city. As a history major the capital cities of Europe, many of them centuries old, are like a treasure trove where dates and facts come alive in the iconic monuments to the greatest, as well as the most tragic, moments of our collective story as nations. Berlin was an eye opener, but not just for what I saw, but rather for what I began to sense in my spirit: parts of the city evidenced the empty shell of Communism with its bleak and impersonal buildings, and I was surprised that you could still feel, palpably, an air of suspicion, fear and depression here, while other areas of the city exuded the pride and dominance of empire. There was a seedy side to the city, too, with its many "adult" stores, so brazenly advertised.

However, it was not the glaring vulgarity of these shops, nor the oppressive atmosphere which clung to the former eastern part of the city, nor even the awe-inspiring splendour of the Brandenburg Gate, which made the strongest impression on me. Far more profoundly impactful was the sense across the city of a wrestle for the growth of small seeds of hope which had been planted audaciously by a generation who had, literally, managed to bring down dividing walls of hostility only a decade ago. Now, ten years after reunification, Berlin had just been made the capital city of this nation and its sparkling, newly renovated parliament building was being unveiled. As I read the words, *Dem Deutschen Volke* ("[To] the German people"), carved above the main façade of the building, I recalled that, throughout the history of this nation, a battle has always raged for the soul of this precious people. Now a new chapter was beginning and this edifice, built in 1894, seemed to encapsulate and still bear witness to this struggle. Kaiser Wilhelm II had tried to block the addition of the inscription because he feared its democratic significance. Where he had failed, the Nazi regime succeeded, and power was wrested from the people into the hands of a fascist dictator. The building itself suffered a fire in 1933, as if symbolizing the hopes and aspirations of the people going up in smoke as the Third Reich quickly stamped out any chance of true freedom, and the building was allowed to fall into disrepair. Here I was now, standing inside the new Bundestag (parliament), wondering whether, this time, the German people would succeed in reversing a curse and redeeming their history.

These were the musings of a young, and very spiritually immature, student! It was not until I started working with Heartcry for Change some ten years later that I began to understand the full spiritual significance of what I had sensed back then in Berlin. Capital cities have an atmosphere all of their own. I began to see that it is in a capital city where you become more acutely aware of how all the contradictions, challenges and prophetic potential of a nation collide. Here they are amplified and focussed, like rays of sun through a magnifying glass, until they ignite a fire. Only a revelation of the battle which rages for them, and the nations they represent, can explain how the same land which counted Bach, Handel, Beethoven, Holbein and many others amongst its sons, could also birth the Nazi Reich with all its atrocities for example. Being part of prayer teams, I have learned that it is the role, and privilege, of the Church to ensure that capital cities burn with revival fire and reformation, rather than the destructive inferno of an enemy who delights to derail the plans of God for a nation by bringing natural and spiritual government out of alignment. In Germany this battle has been more overt but I have discovered that sometimes the enemy's tactics are much more subtle and involve a long war of attrition.

Each time God speaks to us about adopting a nation in prayer or missions I find it is helpful to go and pray in the capital city of the land. As Helen prayed in the newly reformed Berlin God awakened her love for the German nation. She could sense the conflict of their history still wrestling with Germany's calling as a Father Nation in Europe. However, the devil had sabotaged this mandate and used Germany to abuse Europe rather than be its shepherd. I believe that just as people carry destiny and purpose, so do nations and their attributes are best seen in the capital of the nation. Since the capital is a place of authority and government this is the place from which the essence of the nation is established; it is also the place from which conflict and political power control the land. If this government and influence in the capital becomes disconnected from its Kingdom purpose then the nation will never fulfil its God-given mandate. This is why capitals need our prayer.

Part of our commitment as Heartcry for Change to the United States is that we take time to pray in Washington DC. Every six to nine months, we spend 5 days prayer walking Capitol Hill and asking God to give wisdom to its leaders. I discovered on one of these prayer trips that there is a unique pressure which bears down upon those who live and work in capital cities, not least those who are in positions of leadership. I will never forget being part of a team which had been given the privilege of praying for senators and congressmen across the spectrum of political allegiances. On one such occasion, the senator, a Democrat, had agreed to see us, clearly expecting that the group was lobbying for some cause but deciding he should give us time anyway. He was amazed when we told him that we were (mainly American) Christians and that we didn't want anything from him but had in fact come to ask if we might have the honour of praying for him. He was even more intrigued that two of us were from Oxford, England, and were there simply to bless America. Quickly the senator relaxed and agreed to let us pray for him.

One of our team, a wonderful African American pastor, began to sing the hymn Amazing Grace. Instantly the atmosphere in that office changed and the senator began to weep. He then shared with us that he had been in incredible pain with a shoulder injury but that this had only been the latest affliction in a long category of things which had gone wrong for him and his family since he had taken up office and moved to Washington. His house, back in his home state, had been broken into several times, leaving his wife and children vulnerable. His son's best friend had committed suicide leaving his son lonely at school, a close family member had been diagnosed with cancer... and so the list went on. This man was not a Christian but was God fearing and clearly spiritually sensitive as he described feeling like "all hell had broken loose" against him since he had moved to take up his position in the capital. It was such a humbling experience as this leader poured out his heart. Many of our team realized that, so often, we had fallen into the trap of party politics and been blinded to the fact that no man or woman can bear the weight of office in natural government on their own. We need to stand behind them, lifting up their arms with our support and encouragement, so that they might be positioned for success for the good of our nations.

Since that encounter I have loved being part of prayer teams in London, Ankara (Turkey) and Chisinau (Moldova). Each time it has been amazing to see how God reveals the stronghold of a nation through its capital but how these cities also contain the prophetic blueprint and DNA of their respective nation's destiny. There is nothing quite like staking the ground and securing the foundations of a capital city!

SPEAK TO YOUR CITY

As Nehemiah read the report he was given he would have noticed that there were two distinct issues in the account. There was an assessment of the state of the people of God and an analysis of the city. As we have noted, Nehemiah took this report to heart and he prayed and then acted on behalf of both the people and the city. This same distinction is echoed in other places in scripture and is seen here in Isaiah:

> "Because I love Zion, I will not keep still. Because my heart yearns for Jerusalem, I cannot remain silent. I will not stop praying for her until her righteousness shines like the dawn, and her salvation blazes like a burning torch. The nations will see your righteousness. World leaders will be captivated by your glory. And you will be given a new name by the LORD's own mouth." (Isaiah 62:1-3 NLT)

Here the prophet Isaiah speaks out His love for the church and his city.

From Nehemiah and Isaiah we see that, once God infects your heart with a love for your people and nation, doing nothing about your city is no longer an option. You are stirred – you weep – you shout – but you need to make a sound of change. Isaiah expresses that because of his love for the church, he cannot just sit still. Like Isaiah we should feel this passion: "I have to rouse myself – there needs to be movement. My heart is aching". Then the prophet continues, "because I have a heart connection to my city, I cannot be silent". The prophet recognizes that he is living in a critical time for his nation and it is not appropriate to just be silent.

In the same way I believe that God is asking us to break through our sound barriers of fear and speak out. This speaking is not about campaigning for our personal or political agendas but this is communicating the heart of God. This is the cry of prayer, declaring the promises of God for your city and nation until people begin to see it fulfilled. This is a talking time and we must take time to speak to our Jerusalem.

WAKE UP AND ENGAGE

> *"Wake up, wake up, O Zion! Clothe yourself with strength. Put on your beautiful clothes, O holy city of Jerusalem for unclean and godless people will enter your gates no longer. Rise from the dust, O Jerusalem. Sit in a place of honour. Remove the chains of slavery from your neck, O captive daughter of Zion." (Isaiah 52:1-2)*

We read this strong challenge to Zion, which represents the Church, and to the capital city Jerusalem. If the Church is asleep then the city will be godless. Here we see that the Church had been asleep and lost her strength and so Jerusalem had become a godless place without any authority or protection. The prophet Isaiah then called God's people to wake up and take their position so that Jerusalem could again find her place.

I believe that God is calling us prophetically, as the Church in the nations, to take our place. It is time to wake up! In this time of financial and political instability in so many nations, we need to be alert. It is not a good time to be passive and sleeping. God is asking us as His Church to be aware of the season in which we are living. In Hebrews we read this passage:

> "At that time his voice shook the earth, but now he has promised, 'Once more I will shake not only the earth but also the heavens.' The words 'once more' **indicate the removing of what can be shaken – that is, created things – so that what cannot be shaken may remain.** Therefore, since we are receiving a kingdom that cannot be shaken, let us be thankful, and so worship God acceptably with reverence and awe, for our 'God is a consuming fire'." (Hebrews 12:26-29)

These times of shaking are also times of revelation. Why do I say that? Well, this scripture shows us that in all the insecurity the true foundations are being revealed. Everything that can be shaken is being shaken to reveal what our house is built upon, whether the house of our nation or individually. All will be uncovered and exposed. The hidden places will be known. The shaking shows us how we have built. But we do not need to fear. This should be our time of gratitude to our God who is faithful and mighty. We receive this season giving thanks and worshipping our Father who is an amazing God! This is a time of opportunity to shape the future of our culture but we need to engage and pray for our "Jerusalem" as she shakes.

FIRM FOUNDATIONS

The revelation of true foundations happens in times of difficulty. Recently we have had major floods in the Oxford area, where we live, and just like the parable in Luke describes, everything that was not built correctly is exposed when the floods come. We read this biblical account as follows:

> "He is like a man building a house, who dug down deep and laid the foundation on rock. When a flood came, the torrent struck that

> *house but could not shake it, because it was well built. But the one who hears my words and does not put them into practice is like a man who built a house on the ground without a foundation. The moment the torrent struck that house, it collapsed and its destruction was complete."* *(Luke 6:48-49)*

So how do we discover the real foundations of our nation? As this parable demonstrates, it is in the times of shaking that we uncover the true building blocks upon which our society is now depending. Many of the nations in the Western world were originally based upon biblical values but unfortunately consecutive governments have watered down these principles until we no longer represent God in the heart of our legislation or governments. Now we have an opportunity to be part of a Jesus movement that reforms society so that once again it is founded on the principles of God. We need to consider how the natural government can model what God has commanded us to do. God's foundational values and principles never change – they are non-negotiable. So let us read some of the scriptures which describe these foundations:

> *"He set the earth on its foundations; it can never be moved."* *(Psalm 104:5)*

> *"He raises the poor from the dust and lifts the needy from the ash heap; he seats them with princes and has them inherit a throne of honour. For the foundations of the earth are the Lord's; upon them he has set the world. He will guard the feet of his saints, but the wicked will be silenced in darkness. It is not by strength that one prevails; those who oppose the LORD will be shattered. He will thunder against them from Heaven; the LORD will judge the ends of the earth. "He will give strength to his king and exalt the horn of his anointed."* *(1 Samuel 2:8-10)*

"They know nothing, they understand nothing. They walk about in darkness; all the foundations of the earth are shaken." (Psalm 82:5)

"The king should know that the Jews who came up to us from you have gone to Jerusalem and are rebuilding that rebellious and wicked city. They are restoring the walls and repairing the foundations." (Ezra 4:12)

"Your people will rebuild the ancient ruins and will raise up the age-old foundations; you will be called Repairer of Broken Walls, Restorer of Streets with Dwellings." (Isaiah 58:12)

"For he was looking forward to the city with foundations, whose architect and builder is God." (Hebrews 11:10)

In the following passage in Luke we are challenged that it is our obedience that will make a difference. We read in this verse:

"But the one who hears my words and does not put them into practice is like a man who built a house on the ground without a foundation. The moment the torrent struck that house, it collapsed and its destruction was complete." (Luke 6:49)

But the opposite must also be true. If we do obey and build a house upon God's instruction then whatever the storms and opposition that comes against this house, it will still stand on a secure foundation. But this will require something radical. We need a bold generation who will lay down their lives as pioneers for their nation and build on firm foundations.

PILLARS OF GOVERNMENT

Most people, whether young or old, male or female, Christian or non-Christian have all spoken of their surprise at how hard it was to function effectively in their role within the government. As we have related to different individuals in various positions of government within our political systems, they have all commented on the incredible fatigue and pressure they experienced. Congressmen, Members of Parliament and Senators have all shared their sense of isolation. However, over the years I have been touched by how receptive they are to the offer of prayer support. One member of government stopped us when he noticed we were in the corridors and asked, "Are you the people who come to pray?" When we replied that we were, his eyes filled with tears and he said, "You do not realize how much it means to just have people come with no agenda and care for us – these corridors can be very lonely. Most people let us know how badly we are doing or only come to demand favours and leave us feeling used. Thank you for seeing me as a person. That matters!" We should build real connections with our leaders so that they feel supported. We need to wake up and stand in the gates of our government again and bless our leaders.

If we obey the instructions of Paul to his young mentee, Timothy, we would urgently pray for our leaders and those in places of authority.

> *"I urge, then, first of all, that petitions, prayers, intercession and thanksgiving be made for all people – for kings and all those in authority, that we may live peaceful and quiet lives in all godliness and holiness." (1 Timothy 2:1-2)*

But many of us have a very lax attitude towards praying about political figures. In fact sometimes we even believe that our faith and our politics should not mix! But here Paul says this should be an urgent priority so that we can live and function in a safe environment where our faith can flourish. Good government will create an atmosphere where the gospel can be preached more effectively.

So take some time to learn the names of the leaders who represent you and pray for them. Change the spiritual atmosphere that has been harassing them as they seek to take their position of authority and govern wisely. We need to bring an alignment between our spiritual authority and the natural positions of government representing us. Let Heaven and earth come into agreement. So many politicians, local civic leaders and those in the police force feel overwhelmed and cannot see a solution to the many challenges of modern day society. They are lonely and isolated and it is time for the Church to pray and encourage them.

JUSTICE AND RIGHTEOUSNESS

At the root of government you will find two basic motivational values – either justice or righteousness – which influence our policies and beliefs. In fact most political parties tend to reflect one of these attributes more strongly than the other. The conservative or right wing parties are more rooted on the philosophies of what is right or moral. They will have strong policies relating to family life, abortion issues, looking at the principles of personal responsibility and financial independence. The more socialist or left wing parties will look at the justice issues and be more concerned with what is fair and gives equal opportunity. They would concentrate on the needs of the poor, the marginalized, and be concerned with welfare programmes, education and health issues, giving assistance to those less fortunate in society whatever their personal life choices. In our political systems we only seem able to reflect one of these core moral values fully. However, in the Kingdom of God we see both justice and righteousness balanced together to bring perfect government. In the following scriptures we read a description of these two qualities and how they work together:

*"**Righteousness and justice** are the foundation of your throne; love and faithfulness go before you." (Psalm 89:14)*

"Praise be to the LORD your God, who has delighted in you and placed you on the throne of Israel. Because of the Lord's eternal

love for Israel, he has made you king, to maintain **justice and righteousness.**" *(1 Kings 10:9)*

"The Almighty is beyond our reach and exalted in power; in **his justice and great righteousness**, he does not oppress." *(Job 37:23)*

"He will judge the world in **righteousness**; he will govern the peoples with **justice.**" *(Psalm 9:8)*

"Of the increase of his government and peace there will be no end. He will reign on David's throne and over his kingdom, establishing and upholding it with justice and righteousness from that time on and forever. The zeal of the LORD Almighty will accomplish this. **Righteousness and justice** are the foundation of your throne; love and faithfulness go before you." *(Psalm 89:14)*

"In love a throne will be established; in faithfulness a man will sit on it – one from the house of David – one who in judging seeks **justice** and speeds the cause of **righteousness.**" *(Isaish 16:5)*

RIGHTEOUSNESS

Literally it represents: virtue – morality – uprightness – honesty and decency. It results from a right relationship between God and a person, or God and a whole community. Translators have utilized the word "righteousness" when interpreting several different biblical words into English: *sedaqah*, *sedeq*, in the Hebrew; and *dikaiosune* and *euthutes* in the Greek. "Righteousness" in these original languages had a far more spiritual dependence than in our normal English usage today. We understand righteousness to mean "uprightness" in the sense of "an adherence or conformity to an established norm." However, in the original usage, righteousness is rooted in covenants and relationships. For biblical readers, righteousness is primarily the fulfilment of the terms of a covenant between God and humanity.

Basically it is the gift we receive as we willingly position ourselves in an attitude that maintains a right relationship with God. As a result of this relationship you understand and desire to express the ways and values of God and so you then choose to act in a certain way. Thus righteousness carries this deep sense of right and wrong. You need to have an understanding of boundaries, truths and an ability to make "right" choices. Righteousness requires us to have a sense of judgment and take actions that bring about correct alignments.

JUSTICE

This is the understanding of fairness, impartiality and even-handedness. This is the order God seeks to re-establish in His creation where all people receive the benefits of life with Him. As love is the central theme for the New Testament, so justice is the central ethical idea of the Old Testament.

Justice has two major aspects.

1. The standard by which penalties are assigned for breaking the obligations of the society.

2. The standard by which the advantages of social life are handed out, including material goods, rights of participation, opportunities, and liberties.

Justice is the standard for both punishment and benefits and thus can be spoken of as a plumb line.

"I shall use justice as a plumb-line and righteousness as a plummet". (Isaiah 28:17, REB)

Justice has a strong need for compassion. It needs a heart for the marginalized and those of poorer and socially disadvantaged families. Justice sees all the people and cares for them all.

JUSTICE AND RIGHTEOUSNESS IN POLITICS

As we understand these qualities of justice and righteousness more fully, we can then appreciate the challenge it is to express them together in our political institutions. But as the Church we are to take these heavenly principles of government and establish them in our human constructs. Usually if we have a more righteousness with a lesser sense of justice focus, we will tend to have a political stance that is more right wing, with a strong moral fibre that holds fast to good values and principles. However, it often lacks a strong concern or compassion for the poor and the socially marginalized, especially if their poverty is a result of their poor moral choices. So you have a more structured type of government with a strong sense of right and wrong and little margin for error.

But if, on the other hand, we are more justice-oriented, with a lesser sense of righteousness, we will tend to have a political view that is more left wing. It will have a philosophy with a strong ethical sense that people are important and their care and welfare is paramount whatever the choices they have made in life. It will offer a compassionate government style with many social programmes and financial aid for anyone, without distinguishing on the grounds of lifestyle choices. However, these types of government will have weak guidelines of what is right and wrong. It will be a permissive style of government with little understanding of personal accountability.

PRAYING DURING ELECTIONS

Neither of these ideologies fully represents the breadth of the biblical heart. God loves us and is compassionate towards all He has made but He loves us enough to challenge the way we live and correct our poor choices with discipline. Until we get to Heaven and live under God's Kingdom government, we will always have to compromise when choosing our political party on earth. So we will make concessions at some level between righteousness and justice when we vote for our political parties as no one party seems to be able to build with both these principles balanced in a biblical way: either they will have a world view which lacks a compassionate heart towards the poor but has strong traditional moral values, or a more compassionate system towards the poor that does not challenge the areas of morality and personal accountability. This clash of values has often meant well-meaning Christians have opted out of politics and not prayed for their government or the political parties. But we must stand and pray for our leaders and, I believe, engage in the political process even though its values are often flawed and ask for wisdom during election times. There will never be a "perfect choice" but there can be "God's choice" of an individual for the relevant position. So pray during election times that the right men and women will emerge. Ask that every hidden agenda, any corruption or malpractice, will be exposed and that a God-fearing representative will be elected. Once elected, support your leaders even if you did not vote for them. Pray for these elected men and women and ask God to strengthen our leaders in these tough times of political shaking.

CONNECTION TIME

My call to London, my capital city, started one morning when I woke up singing the song – "Let me take you by the hand and walk you through the streets of London" – as I described in the previous chapter. This was a profound spiritual moment when God challenged me to take responsibility for my nation and city. I had grown up as a child in India and once married had worked in Africa, so Britain did not "feel" like my nation. I had struggled to connect to my English roots and, if I'm honest, I had resisted them. I was still very intimidated by this different culture and the vast metropolis of London. However, this day changed my life. I responded to the challenge of this song and went to London. When I looked into the eyes of the many ordinary people pushing their way along the pavements I realized that this was my city and these people were my flesh and blood and I melted.

The hardness of my heart yielded and a deep love for this place filled me. I would never be the same. Since this first time I have returned to pray in London many times. I love the privilege of walking in my city. The atmosphere in some areas is still oppressive and intimidating but I continue to walk the streets of London. Whether through Mayfair, Westminster and the halls of power or around Hackney, Tower Hamlets and the boroughs of deprivation, I have allowed this city to become part of me. I have walked the streets in the day and I have also walked them at night. In fact I walked the streets of London regularly for a period of three months until they became imprinted into my spirit. London is still in my heart today: I cannot help but cry out to God for my capital city, my government and leaders and my nation. What about you – will you carry your capital and bless your nation?

LONDON LEGACY

As we celebrated the 20th anniversary of Heartcry I wanted to mark the occasion with a time of 3 days of prayer. I considered travelling to many nations with a team to pray but no destination seemed to resonate and the arrangements fell through. Finally, as we prayed once again about what we should do, God reminded us that Heartcry had started with a profound encounter as we prayed on the streets of London. All those years ago when I had walked and prayed and visited the sites of past revivals, God had mandated us to watch over this capital city. He then spoke to us and said, "Now it is time to stake this ground again". So we took a team of intercessors from several different nations, Egypt, Norway, Sweden, England and the USA and decided to bless London and call out her prophetic destiny together once again.

We chose the Churchill War Rooms as our base and hired a room there. As we walked in, there was an exhibition of the Battle for Britain, explaining Churchill's strategy which had led to victory in the Second World War. Playing over the loud speakers was a recording of

Churchill's radio broadcast to the other European nations and, as his voice was heard announcing "this is London calling!", we felt the cry of the land – London is calling again! We realized that God is raising up a new generation of people to battle for Britain and stake the ground. A poster on the wall from the war era summarized it perfectly: "Never was so much owed by so many to so few". It is time to take our place and leave a legacy which will bless the next generation.

As if to emphasize this new commission, on two occasions, as we were praying over these three days, we just "happened" to be in the right place at the right time to witness the changing of the guard at Buckingham Palace and Windsor Castle. As we watched this procession, God spoke to us: "This is the time for the changing of the guard!" Although I have used London as my example here I want you to know that these principles apply to your nation and capital too. God is calling you to build connections with your cities and shift and change nations. The Holy Spirit impressed on us that this is a new season and that it is critical for us to understand how to stand guard over our nation's capital. Our capitals and nations are calling – are we ready to respond?

Prayer:

Father we thank you for your Kingdom and government. The more we read your Word and then our newspapers the more we realize we need your power and authority in our cities and government. So we pray – Our Father, Let Your Kingdom come and Your will be done on this earth. In our cities and nations we ask that you will establish your throne of justice and righteousness. Please use us to be those who carry the good news of Jesus into the corridors of power. Teach us to support and pray for our leaders in a righteous way. Thank you for our cities and our nation. Let us be faithful to pray for them. Amen.

 Change the World

PRAYING PROPHETIC PRAYERS FROM A TENDER HEART

Prayer is powerful. It can write the capital letter at the beginning of each sentence of history. I believe that as we connect to God and pray in alignment with His heart, we shift and alter the destiny of nations. What a privilege we have to pray. In days of uncertainty and uproar, it is easy to pray "worry prayers", those that just speak of our anxiety, rather than prayers of hope and declaration. We have looked at our devotional life of prayer, studied the place of intercession, and explored the journey of prayer walking and staking this land for Jesus. Now I believe that God wants the Church to become His house of prayer and write history – His story – in these turbulent days.

LET MY PEOPLE GO!

As we look at the nations and discern the atmosphere in our neighbourhoods, a "Moses like" cry should be stirred in our being. We should feel enraged by the enemy's exploitation of people's lives around us. On every side people are gripped by tormenting fears and deep anxiety so how can we remain silent? The Church needs to arise and cry out "Let these people go!" This is a time when we need to declare their deliverance and freedom. Gordon and I have the privilege of connecting with the Betel Organisation which works with those who have become trapped by drug and alcohol addiction. Through the power of prayer, loving discipline and growing healthy relationships they demonstrate that the kindness of Jesus never fails. They are an army of amazing people who are ready to pray and act on behalf of the broken. There is disappointment and hardship, they are mocked and ridiculed, but they have found God never fails. Wherever we live today we are all aware of someone who is broken, maybe depressed and contemplating suicide, going through divorce or struggling with addictions – and they need kindness. God asks us if we will stand with the bruised and wounded and cry out for their lives and help them. We need to start a new Jesus movement and reverse every curse of the devil in our society. But this will take a dedicated, radical group of people who are ready to lay down their lives for the lost. In Jeremiah chapter 30 we read these verses:

> "Ask and see: Can a man bear children? **Then why do I see every strong man with his hands on his stomach like a woman in labour, every face turned deathly pale?** How awful that day will be! None will be like it. It will be a time of trouble for Jacob, but he will be saved out of it. **'In that day,'** declares the LORD Almighty, 'I will break the yoke off their necks and will tear off their bonds; no longer will foreigners enslave them.'" (Jeremiah 30:5-9)

Here we see that desperate times require desperate measures. There is such trouble in the land that the men experience "spiritual birth pains" as they labour in prayer for the freedom of the people. I believe that just as God heard the cry of suffering and was concerned for the Israelites in the book of Exodus, so God hears the groaning of the people under a heavy yoke of slavery today. He calls us to partner with His concerns and cry out for the deliverance of the burdened. There is so much hopelessness and pain all around us; but it is our privilege to hear this cry and break the yokes of their spiritual oppression in prayer. Let us cry freedom and watch God set the captives free!

FROM A TOUGH TO A TENDER HEART

Does the hardship of people's lives affect you? Can you feel the agony of God's heart for His world? Ernest prayer requires us to have a tender heart tuned to both the cry of God and the needs of the people. In Ezekiel we read that one of the benefits of being filled with the Holy Spirit is that He will soften the hardness of our hearts. In this passage of scripture we read as follows:

> "And I will give you a new heart, and I will put a new spirit in you. I will take out your stony, stubborn heart and give you a tender, responsive heart". (Ezekiel 36:26 NLT)

So we need to let God tenderize our hearts towards the community, allow Him to open our ears to their cry, and then teach us to have faith for breakthrough in the lives of our friends and neighbours as we pray. We need the oil of the Holy Spirit to soften our hearts and remove the tough selfishness so that we can reach out beyond our own convenience.

In 1986 we were working in Blantyre, Malawi, with Reinhard Bonnke and the Christ for all Nations team preparing for an evangelistic campaign and I want to share with you the remarkable story of a beggar man who used to sit at the bottom of the stairs to our office. He was a cripple, paralyzed from his hips downwards, and he used to move by dragging himself along the pavements with his arms. Despite his disability, he was often smiling even though it was obvious that he had an extremely hard life. I would see him most days and bring him food and we developed a friendship. Once the meetings started, I asked him if he would like to come with us and hear about Jesus. He agreed and so we took him in our vehicle. That night he received prayer and the power of God went through his body: his legs, usually stone cold, became warm and he began to have feeling in his feet again. However, when he tried to walk he could not. Disappointed he returned home and was back at the bottom of our stairs begging later that week. Certain that this man had had a healing encounter with God, I decided to pray about his situation. The next day a pastor from one of the local churches came to me and said, "I have been praying for your beggar and feel that we need to anoint him with oil for one year". She went on to explain, "This man's limbs are so calloused from being dragged along on the roads that they cannot move because the skin is too hard, but I believe if we will soak his legs in warm oil and massage him every day he will walk again. We just need to remove all the dead skin so that he can move his muscles!" So this is what they did: long after we had left Blantyre for the next mission, this congregation continued to massage this man's legs with oil.

When I returned to Malawi ten years later, I was walking in the market when I heard my name being shouted: "Mama Rachel, Bonnke Lady, Mama Rachel, please stop!" So I stopped and turned around to see a strong man running towards me. "I am your beggar man", he said, "but now my name is Abraham. I am an evangelist and I share the news of Jesus everywhere." He then told me how, after being massaged with warm oil, his legs had begun to move more and more until all the dead hardened skin was removed and now he could walk perfectly.

In the same way I believe God wants to lubricate our toughened selfish hearts with His warm oil, removing all the hardened areas, so that we can arise and walk as a Church with faith and kindness in this hour. For too long our faith and tenderness have been crippled, but God has come to heal us and enable us to walk as children of faith with soft hearts and sensitive hearing. So Church, let us surrender our lives to this warm oil of His Spirit and be healed! We need to be a listening Church so that we can pray the effective prayers of faith from the heart of our Father.

THE VALLEY OF DRY BONES

Can our nations live again? Can we see Jesus reflected in our communities as we begin to pray? As we cry out we are speaking to the land. We are declaring His promises and calling forth the destiny of the people and the land. We are not just praying our thoughts but declaring God's word. We need to prophesy to the land and bring a supernatural alignment on earth as we pray. We can observe this process between God and His prophet in Ezekiel 37, so let us read this passage:

"The hand of the LORD was on me, and he brought me out by the Spirit of the LORD and set me in the middle of a valley; it was full of bones. He asked me, 'Son of man, can these bones live?' I said, 'Sovereign LORD, you alone know'. Then he said to me, 'Prophesy to these bones and say to them, 'Dry bones, hear the word of the LORD!' This is what the Sovereign LORD says to these bones: 'I will make breath enter you, and you will come to life. I will attach tendons to you and make flesh come upon you and cover you with skin; I will put breath in you, and you will come to life. Then you will know that I am the LORD.'

So I prophesied as I was commanded. And as I was prophesying, there was a noise, a rattling sound, and the bones came together, bone to bone. I looked, and tendons and flesh appeared on them and skin covered them, but there was no breath in them.

Then he said to me, 'Prophesy to the breath; prophesy, son of man, and say to it, 'This is what the Sovereign LORD says: Come, breath, from the four winds and breathe into these slain, that they may live.' So I prophesied as he commanded me, and breath entered them; they came to life and stood up on their feet – a vast army.

Then he said to me: 'Son of man, these bones are the people of Israel. They say, 'Our bones are dried up and our hope is gone; we are cut off.' Therefore prophesy and say to them: 'This is what the Sovereign LORD says: My people, I am going to open your graves and bring you up from them; I will bring you back to the land of Israel. Then you, my people, will know that I am the LORD, when I open your graves and bring you up from them. I will put my Spirit in you and you will live, and I will settle you in your own land. Then you will know that I the LORD have spoken, and I have done it, declares the LORD.'" (Ezekiel 37:1-14)

SPEAK TO THE BONES

God asks his prophet, "Can these bones live?" – in other words, what potential can you see for hope in this situation? Similarly, I believe God is asking us as we pray, "Can the bones of our broken communities be revived?" As we walk our streets, we need to see beyond the hopelessness and capture God's vision for restoration. We need to carry God's prophetic cry as we pray. Ezekiel responds cautiously stating that only God knows the true outcome and how this situation can turn around. But God asks his prophet to act, he commands him to speak and release the breath of life. Likewise, now prophesy and allow your voice to shake every desolate situation.

God is asking us to see beyond the mere statistics of our society and declare a word of hope to every shattered life. As we begin to speak, we will start a movement of transformation. Something will shift and change in the spirit. The stifling atmospheres of depression and negativity will have to leave. The dry bones of Ezekiel will be transformed into a mighty army. The desperate cry of our neighbourhoods can change into sounds of joy. God answers when we pray. Recently I preached at a national conference in the north of England. Before I spoke, I had such a sense that it was time for a shift in our nation and that people need to see Jesus touch their lives in a time of hopelessness. So I asked God for a sign that Jesus was coming to our nation. Here is the story of what happened:

I spoke a message entitled "Consider Jesus" on the Saturday morning and asked people to respond and make Jesus the priority and centre of their life. One of those who responded was a lady and she told me this story: Her son had left home three years earlier and run off to London. However, two weeks ago she heard from this son that he was now connected with a church called St Barnabas and they had taken him to the New Wine summer camp. (This is the church my brother and his family attend). There he had then joined the youth as part of their skateboarding team. On the Thursday, whilst away on this Christian camp, he gave his life to Jesus. This mother was so surprised that her son, who was violently anti anything to do with God, would make such a radical decision. However, she had now come away for the weekend to visit a long-time friend of hers in Lincoln. She soon discovered that this close friend had also given her life to Jesus and joined a church. Perplexed she agreed to go with her friend to a summer conference called One Event for their Saturday morning meeting in a Big Top circus tent with 5,000 other people. Here she heard me speak and responded with tears crying, "I now get it. You opened the door for me. I never knew I needed God or that He wanted to help me!", and she too gave her life to Jesus! Here in one family, my brother's church rescued and helped the son in London and God allowed me to touch his mother in Lincoln, in the north of England. The angels must have been busy in the coordination department that day! It makes me love Jesus even more. What a joy to serve Him! When we pray and prophesy to the dry bones, miracles will happen. Families will be healed and restored.

PROPHETIC NOT PATHETIC PRAYER!
As we begin to pray with a tender heart and sensitive ears, we will begin to echo the heart cry of God. Prophetic intercession is the

prayer that captures the voice of God for a person or community and then speaks. As we learn to recognize the spiritual season around us more accurately, our spirit becomes attuned to the purpose of God so we can work with Him more effectively. We need to be like Jesus, those who can truly say – all that I do only reflects what I see my Father doing in Heaven.

Prophetic prayer is where you have an urge, prompted by the Holy Spirit, to pray for a situation about which you can have very little natural knowledge. You find you pray the requests of God. He prompts you to pray so that you can intervene and stand in the gap with His word. This type of prayer depends upon good two way communication between yourself and God. This is where you hear the heart of God by revelation and then you speak back to God about the situation in prayer. Prophetic prayer is not the prayer triggered on earth by the lists of people's needs and circumstances, but rather this prayer is prompted by revelation from Heaven which focusses your prayer towards a particular issue. This type of prayer requires you to listen to God before you pray. You need to take time to wait, listen, and then speak. For example, you may feel that you need to pray for the nations. First take some time and ask God which nation and then ask which particular area of the nation- should it be a geographical area or a functional area like education?

Prophetic prayer often has a strong authoritative declaration as you are calling God's word into the situation, not just your requests. You literally become God's mouthpiece, allowing His word to flow through you. God aligns our mouths with His and we speak His word into situations and shift circumstances because the power is in His word even though it is spoken through our mouth. So what are the cries of the heart of God for our nations at this time? What should the Church be hearing and praying? Let us explore some of the different areas that God is highlighting in this season.

HARVEST TIME – TIME TO BE SAVED!

All over the world there is a growing hunger to know about God. People need the Lord and they are curious. First we need to talk to God about our friends and then we can talk to them about God, knowing that their heart is already prepared ground. We are living in days of great opportunity but we need to act.

> **"In that day** I will restore David's fallen tent. I will repair its broken places, restore its ruins, and build it as it used to be,12 so that they may possess the remnant of Edom and all the nations that bear my name, " declares the LORD, who will do these things.13 **"The days are coming," declares the LORD, "when the reaper will be overtaken by the ploughman and the planter by the one treading grapes**. New wine will drip from the mountains and flow from all the hills." (Amos 9:11-13)

When scripture uses this phrase, "in that day" or "in the fullness of time", we need to recognize that these phrases denote an encounter moment when "chronos", the time on earth, aligns with "kairos", the eternal time of Heaven, and God breaks through. So here the prophet Amos is speaking about one of these expected instances. On "that day" there will be a rapid harvest and a restoration of the Church and we will see an acceleration of fruitfulness in all our work. Suddenly we will find that we will be reaping the harvest faster than we can sow the seed. We will see the legacy and investment of the past prayers and promises flourish and it will be a time to touch and see the reality of our hope materializing. What a wonderful day! But at the moment we are not living in the fullness of "that Day" so we still need to live in the "THIS" day of pre-harvest, and these days demand hard work. We need to work in the season of tears before the joy; we need to labour in the days of sowing before reaping. So this is the season to release the prophetic cry for harvest, crying out for change in our generation, government and society, knowing that God has promised to visit us. We will see souls saved, prodigals return to Jesus and many crying out for knowledge of God. We have sown in tears for the many precious people we love and those seeds of prayer are not wasted. This is a time to declare salvation will come to our house and they will be saved!

CRY FOR JUSTICE AND TRUTH

As we stand with God and watch over our cities and communities we can sense God's heart for the marginalized. God hears the cries of distress in our land. All around us is the injustice of slave trafficking, sexual abuse and poverty. Violence, addictions and broken marriages bring confusion and pain into many homes as little children struggle to find a place of safety. God is not indifferent to this suffering. In these following scriptures we see the priority that God gives to these justice issues in our land and we need to echo His cry:

> "Do not mistreat an alien or oppress him, for you were aliens in Egypt. Do not take advantage of a widow or an orphan. If you do and they cry out to me, I will certainly hear their cry." (Exodus 22:22-23)

> "Then you will call, and the LORD will answer; you will cry for help, and he will say: 'Here am I'. If you do away with the yoke of oppression, with the pointing finger and malicious talk, and if you spend yourselves in behalf of the hungry and satisfy the needs of the oppressed, then your light will rise in the darkness, and your night will become like the noonday." (Isaiah 58:9-11)

So we need to come and be the voice for the voiceless, for those who are suffering in our nations. God hears their cry and we need to speak out on their behalf. We need to be ready to confront the mistreatment of children, the neglect of the older widows and the poor. We need to be voices that bring relief and freedom for those who have been forsaken.

We need to cry out:

> "**Lift up your heads, O you gates**; be lifted up, you ancient doors, that the King of glory may come in. Who is this King of glory? The LORD strong and mighty, the LORD mighty in battle. Lift up your heads, O you gates; lift them up, you ancient doors, that the King of glory may come in." (Psalm 24:7-9)

We need to pray that the "gates", the places of authority in our communities, will make room for Kingdom principles and priorities to be supported by governmental institutions. We need to release a prophetic cry from the Church that we want to see righteous authority, balanced with justice, to sit in the gates of finance, commerce, education, social culture, health and media. We want to welcome the Kingdom attitudes into every area of governmental and community life. We need to cry out for a new culture of kindness and justice to serve our neighbourhoods. It is time for the oppressor to go and peace to come to our streets and homes.

CRY "IN WRATH REMEMBER MERCY!"

Since God is sovereign you may wonder if it is worth investing so much time in prayer for the nations and governments. Surely God has decided what He will do, so does it make any difference? But if we examine the lives of the prophets, we find that all of them were intercessors for their nations in times of crisis. We are familiar with the famous prophetic cry of Habakkuk, "Oh God in wrath remember mercy!" We read that Daniel fasted and prayed for his nation for 21 days, engaging in an intense spiritual battle. We also know the story of Jonah who was sent on assignment as a prophet to the great city of Nineveh where he was told to preach against it because its wickedness had come to the attention of God. After some reluctance Jonah did go and deliver his message of judgment, and the people's response was not what Jonah expected.

They responded in humility as follows:

> "Who knows? God may yet relent and with compassion turn from his fierce anger so that we will not perish. When God saw what they did and how they turned from their evil ways, he had compassion and did not bring upon them the destruction he had threatened." (Jonah 2:9-10)

So why do I believe that we should pray and release these prophetic cries of intercession? Can we change the mind of God? I believe that when God says he is coming to a nation, city or person then God keeps His word and will come; however I believe we can determine **the way in which He comes** through our prayers. Will God come in mercy or judgment? God has promised us that "He who is coming will come", so we had better get ready! We may not be able to alter the timing of God, but I do believe He will hear our cry and may adjust the way in which He comes to visit us if we will cry out.

So let us cry out for our nations. Surely as we look around us we can see the godlessness. We know that we deserve the wrath of God but let us touch Heaven with a cry of mercy and watch what our God will do for us.

PROMISES OF REVIVAL

As you begin to pray, you find that God will often remind you of prophetic words or scriptures concerning the situation. I remember when I first returned to the UK in 1990 I often found myself praying Isaiah 60 verses 1-3 over the nation. I felt God say that this scripture, "Arise and shine", was a declaration calling forth His glory over our nation. God wanted us to arise and be glory carriers who would release light into all the darkness in the land. So what are other significant prophetic words that have been given concerning Europe that we can pray?

The original references of the following prophecies can be found at the end of this chapter on page 221.

HUDSON TAYLOR'S VISION, 1855

This vision was received while he was preaching in Britain, on furlough from China.

> *"I have seen a vision. I saw in this vision a great war that encompasses the world. I saw this war recede and then start again, actually being two wars. After this I saw much unrest and revolts that will affect many nations. I saw in some places spiritual awakenings. In Russia I saw there will come a general all-encompassing national spiritual awakening spread to many European countries. Then I saw an all-out awakening, followed by the coming of Christ."*

THE MOTHER BARBARA PROPHECY, 1911

In 1918, shortly before Mother Barbara went to live in the community house near the Garden of Gethsemane on the Mount of Olives in Jerusalem, she was given a prophecy by Bishop Aristocoli of the Russian Orthodox Church which he had received in 1911 while in prayer. Some of the events foreseen in this remarkable prophecy have already been fulfilled. The rise and fall of communism in Russia has taken place. Germany was divided in two for nearly fifty years from 1945. Britain has lost her empire and her colonies. This must have seemed impossible back in 1911 before the First World War when Britain ruled the largest empire the world had ever known and was the richest and most powerful nation. The prophecy was first published in Prophecy Today in September 1986, soon after the Carmel Gathering, where it was prophesied that the Soviet Union was about to fall. The storm clouds were already gathering over the USSR:

> *"Tell the women they must belong absolutely to God. They must believe in the great things that are happening and that God is doing on the earth. They must prepare their souls, their children and their husbands. And they will have very much work*

to do for God. Oh, what a great work the women will have to do in the end time, and the men will follow them. NOT ONE COUNTRY WILL BE WITHOUT TRIAL – do not be frightened by anything you will hear.

An evil will shortly take Russia and wherever this evil comes, rivers of blood will flow. This evil will take the whole world and wherever it goes, rivers of blood will flow because of it. It is not the Russian soul, but an imposition on the Russian soul. It is not an ideology, or a philosophy, but a spirit from hell. In the last days Germany will be divided in two. France will just be nothing. Italy will be judged by natural disasters. Britain will lose her empire and all her colonies and will come to almost total ruin, but will be saved by praying women. America will feed the world, but will finally collapse. Russia and China will destroy each other. Finally, Russia will be free, and from her believers will go forth and turn many from the nations to God."

THE GREAT REVIVAL – SMITH WIGGLESWORTH

This prophecy was given at the annual Elim conference in 1947:

"During the next few decades there will be two distinct moves of the Holy Spirit across the church in Great Britain. The first move will affect every church that is open to receive it and will be characterised by a restoration of the baptism and gifts of the Holy Spirit. The second move of the Holy Spirit will result in people leaving historic churches and planting new churches. In the duration of each of these moves, the people involved will say, 'This is a great revival'. But the Lord says, 'No, neither is the great revival but both are steps towards it'. When the new church phase is on the wane, there will be evidenced in the churches something that has not been seen before: a coming together of those with an emphasis on the Word and those with

an emphasis on the Spirit. When the Word and the Spirit come together, there will be the biggest movement of the Holy Spirit that the nation, indeed the world, has even seen. It will mark the beginning of a revival that will eclipse anything that has been witnessed within these shores, even the Wesleyan and the Welsh revivals of former years. The outpouring of God's Spirit will flow over from the United Kingdom to the mainland of Europe, and from there will begin a missionary move to the ends of the earth."

A MESSAGE FROM JEAN DARNALL – 24 FEB 2005

"Recently I have sensed that Christians will be called to the market place as witnesses where people work. They will be sent into ordinary professions and enabled by the Holy Spirit to do extra-ordinary things that will cause unbelievers to recognize God's power and word in our world today. There will be Christian leaders with unusual creativity and originality, based on biblical truth and dependant upon spiritual gifts. They will affect the culture; 'the why' and 'the how' people will do business, govern, educate and entertain will be changed.

The world's image of the church in the twenty-first century will not be of people hidden in the pews inside of traditional church edifices. They will become recognized as the church in the workplace, visible witnesses; individuals whose public worship (service) will cause change. In Jan. 2000 I had a strong witness during prayer of how the persecution of Christians will intensify all through the twenty-first century. The scope of persecution will be increased to the world-wide church. Perilous and challenging times are coming upon Christians in England and USA.

The instruction that came to me was, 'Prepare the people for *persecution'. There will be enemies within and without the church. Islam and a secular society will target Christianity as 'the enemy' and attack with a vicious hatred. Persecution will purify many believers to live for God and cause them to seek the Spirit's power. It will also force them, because of the attacks upon their institutions, to move their witness to their workplaces, and thus spread their message and ministry. Tumultuous, troubled times will shock and stir up believers. Some will fall away in fear, but others will stand taller than they have ever done before. Boldness will increase as the persecution increases all through the century."*

As we read these various prophetic words it is easy to recognize the truths in the message and the many parts of these words that have already happened. But then as we consider what still remains to be fulfilled we find these words demand a response and accountability from us, the Church of today. Many times in scripture we read a description of what the social, climatic and economic situations will be like in the "last days" and so we should not be alarmed. In Matthew 24:4-25 we read an account of what will happen in the nations and the attitude towards the Church. In verse 6 Jesus states that "these things must happen but the end is still to come!" So as we pray I do not believe that we can pray to stop every disaster and decline but we can pray that as the Church we will be prepared and be the voice of Jesus in the midst of these unusual days. Watch and pray over the nations and, like Jesus, let us declare that we want to do the will of God, whatever the cost, in the times ahead.

LIVING IN A GARDEN OF BEAUTY

As you read this following passage from Ezekiel 36, you can hear the sound of God's redemptive heart towards communities and nations. God will take the desolate places and make them fruitful again:

"This is what the Sovereign Lord says: 'On the day I cleanse you from all your sins, I will resettle your towns, and the ruins will be rebuilt. The desolate land will be cultivated instead of lying desolate in the sight of all who pass through it.' They will say, 'This land that was laid waste has become like the garden of Eden; the cities that were lying in ruins, desolate and destroyed, are now fortified and inhabited.' 'Then the nations around you that remain will know that I the Lord have rebuilt what was destroyed and have replanted what was desolate. I the Lord have spoken, and I will do it.' This is what the Sovereign Lord says: 'Once again I will yield to Israel's plea and do this for them: I will make their people as numerous as sheep, as numerous as the flocks for offerings at Jerusalem during her appointed festivals. So will the ruined cities be filled with flocks of people? Then they will know that I am the Lord'." (Ezekiel 36:33-38)

Often we find our life journey is like that described above: we have the promise of a fertile landscape but find ourselves in a wilderness place with little hope; but through prayer and faith we can press through and find a garden. This passage expresses it like this: "This land that was laid waste has become like the Garden of Eden". As you pray, let this thought stir you – let the barren desolate places of people's lives and the nations be transformed and become a garden once again. Prophesy to the people and the land and let this be a turning time in our generation. Isaiah and Jeremiah prophesy about this change – a time when the wilderness changes from desolation into a fertile, productive garden. The Bible starts with mankind living in a garden, knowing the care of God daily and fruitfulness of harvest all around them. I believe that God wants to restore hope once again, whatever the pain and ruins we see around us today, God has a purpose, and He desires, with us, to see every curse of evil turned for good in the lives of our communities and cities. God is fighting for us and He has spoken by His word.

THE WHOLE WORLD COVERED WITH THE GLORY OF GOD

> *"And the glory of the LORD will be revealed, and all people will see it together. For the mouth of the LORD has spoken."* *(Isaiah 40:5)*

> *"For the earth will be filled with the knowledge of the glory of the LORD as the waters cover the sea."* *(Habakkuk 2:14)*

The glory and presence of God will become evident and people will become aware that God is in the land. Often, when we least expect it, we hear that God is here. All over the Middle East at this time there is a rumour – that the "man in white" is appearing to the broken, sick and dying. This Man comes as a bright light and talks to them of hope and healing. They ask one another in the market squares, "Have you seen Him yet?" The glory of God is being revealed. Many thousands are finding Jesus as they pray in their homes and mosques – Jesus is revealing Himself. One thing we know for certain: when all is said and done, Jesus triumphs – He wins the day! We know that the prayers and travail of His heart will be satisfied. Every prayer that Jesus has cried for us will be fulfilled. We will win. We will see the promise of our labour. God will come!

I love prayer because it is this key that moves the hand of God to write a story of His presence in the nations. Prayer is this special place where we connect to the heart of God and then change the world. As we find our fluency and language, and become a friend of God, we shift heavenly atmospheres and see His promises established on the earth. The manifest presence of God will rest on our lives and communities. I do not know why *you* pray, but I love to hear the stories of lives changed, people envisioned and hope awakened; but more than the answers to prayer, I love prayer. I love the incredible privilege we have to talk to God and become His friend.

So let us pray:

Father – what a privilege it is to talk with the living God. What an amazing journey it is to walk and talk with you. Teach us to pray – Teach us to LOVE prayer – Teach us to change our world and open up Heaven and see your power released. Let your revelation and instruction increase in our lives. Show us how to be those who know and reveal the heart of God to others. Let us be part of a Jesus movement in our days. Thank you for this honour of talking with You. Amen.

References for prophetic words in this chapter

All of these prophetic words are well documented and appear on several websites. The first three (Hudson Taylor, Mother Barbara and Smith Wigglesworth) were also cited in the January/February 2000 edition of Prophecy Today. Jean Darnall's words for the UK can be found, amongst other places, at the following website:

http://freesites.ourchurch.com/p/PropheticAnointingUK/?page_id=84

Appendix 1 – Aids to Prayer

There are many aids to prayer I could discuss, but here I have listed just a few suggestions you might want to consider:

- Banners with topics
- Mission's newsletters/bulletins
- Maps of your local area
- A globe or flags of the nations
- Photographs of family members
- Testimonies
- Going prayer walking in your neighbourhood
- Forming prayer triplets with a focussed project
- A prayer scrapbook with collection information
- Statistics/newspaper articles
- Prayer requests

These are all tools that can stimulate a broader dimension of prayer. Find out what works for you so that you are able to build your house of prayer. Ask God to breathe new creativity into your prayer life.

Appendix 2 – Manual for Healing Prayer Ministry

SECURING THE MIND-FIELD

> *"He makes me lie down in green pastures, he leads me beside quiet waters, he restores my soul." (Psalm 23:2-3)*

> *"Do not conform any longer to the pattern of this world, but be transformed by the renewing of your mind. Then you will be able to test and approve what God's will is – his good, pleasing and perfect will." (Romans 12:2)*

Soul/spirit hurts are wounds which are deeply personal and internal which require God's healing touch to restore emotional, mental and spiritual wholeness. It is likely that we will encounter the need for this type of healing much more frequently in people we pray for as society and family life become increasingly dysfunctional.

There are many events and circumstances in our lives which can leave us feeling bruised, wounded or even traumatized. They affect our behaviour and mindsets and dictate our responses to present and future situations. They often leave us feeling enslaved by our past, rather than free to live life to the full in the present and with hope in our hearts for the future. Typical hurts, feelings and symptoms associated with such wounds are:

- Fear
- Rejection
- Insecurity
- Defensiveness
- Drivenness
- Inadequacy/lack of self-esteem
- False humility

- Guilt
- Depression
- Abandonment

Some of the causes of these hurts are loss, a traumatic event or accident, early childhood memories of abandonment or separation, abuse, divorce, abortion or violence. The outworking of these hurts can be shame, anger, bitterness, physical conditions, depression, insomnia, anxiety, phobias, mental insanity, secrecy, inability to connect with emotions or cry, demonic oppression and, in extreme cases of ritual Satanic or sexual abuse, dissociation and split personality disorders. In some cases these conditions and afflictions can be traced back through the generations and seem to be something which has dogged our family's history. Although deeply rooted and often complex, none of these situations or their effects is beyond the healing and liberating power of God!

In order to understand how these emotional wounds scar us and affect our day to day life, we need to understand the connection of mind and soul. Our mind is a powerful component of our soul and the soul is the essence of who we are. It is the seat of our will, emotions and belief systems. If, through traumatic events in our lives, we become wounded and scarred, it is often our mind which then becomes a minefield of conflicting and enslaving thoughts. These, if left to take hold, quickly develop into what are known as ungodly beliefs which create thought patterns and mindsets which dictate our reactions, expectations and behaviour. We become trapped and learn to build on the foundations of lies, rather than the truth of God.

EXAMPLES OF CRIPPLING HURTS
Rejection/insecurity
Rejection means: to throw away, push aside, judge as inferior or of a low standard or to refuse entrance.

Many people never lift up their heads as they are listening to the voice of rejection. It may be that we have experienced rejection from birth and life has taught us that we are unwanted and unloved and that we will never be accepted. As this becomes our expectation and dominant thought pattern, we live out life in that role, never expecting to be welcomed, received and appreciated. We may find that our behaviour changes and we reject other people's love before we can be rejected. Our whole belief system is programmed around a deep ungodly belief that we are basically unworthy of love and will always live to the sound of rejection in our lives.

Rejection started speaking to women in the Garden of Eden and continues to plague both men and women today. It is the fundamental lie of the enemy which we must renounce and replace with the truth of God's Word. Compare Genesis 3:1-13 with Psalm 139:13-14.

We need to recognize that we have an enemy and he hates our destiny. We have a deceiver and he is very convincing. Whatever your background, even beautiful, educated and wealthy people can have very real feelings of:

- Insecurity
- Inferiority
- Sense of failure
- Distrust
- Hopelessness
- Rejection – Nobody really loves me
- Intimidation
- Fear
- Unbelief in their abilities

The root of rejection is a root of deception. We have listened to the serpent and believed the lie and the strength of our feelings; we have interpreted our circumstances against this voice and have lost the sound of the Word of God.

As we believe the lies of the enemy, there develops within us what is known as an ungodly belief. As this becomes rooted in our thought patterns we allow rejection to become part of our identity and life experience so the hurt pattern repeats itself as a vicious cycle.

We can only fight this kind of lie and break the cycle by:

- Renouncing the lies- sometimes we will have to help people process memories and instances from their past as they are triggered by the Holy Spirit in order to pull up the lie by its roots.

- Affirming the truth- we need to ensure that we help people recognize and replace the lies they have believed with the truth of what God says about them in Scripture

Fear/intimidation/terror/phobias

"For God did not give us a spirit of fear but of power, love and a sound mind." (2 Timothy 1:7)

"For you did not receive a spirit that makes you a slave again to fear, but you received the Spirit of sonship. And by him we cry, 'Abba, Father'." (Romans 8:15)

Fear and intimidation rob us of our very identity as children of God. When Jesus was tempted in the wilderness, the devil questioned this core fact and tried to sow the lie that Jesus wasn't who God had proclaimed and affirmed Him to be at His baptism, "My beloved Son in whom I delight".

Some common fears are:

- Fear of man
- Irrational fears
- Fear of death

- Fear of the future
- Fear of punishment/condemnation
- Fear of sickness
- Fear of finances
- Fear of abandonment

All of these call into question elements of God's provision, care and promises for our lives. Their outworking is:

- Self-protection
- Isolation
- Control
- Guardedness
- Inability to trust
- Anxiety/stress
- Anger

We must be ruthless in rooting out the fears that control us and live in the carefree awareness of our adoption into God's family. Other key strongholds which give ground to ungodly belief systems can be grouped together as follows:

- Anger/bitterness/unforgiveness/jealousy
- Guilt and shame

As we pray for people we must try to discern the root of a problem rather than attack its fruit. Be aware for example that not all anger is a problem with self-control but might be rooted in fear, terror or rejection and be a well developed self-defense mechanism. It is essential that we don't make assumptions about people, but ask the Holy Spirit for wisdom and revelation as we pray. Once we have identified the core issue and uprooted the controlling lie we can apply the medicine of the Word of God and affirm the truth to replace the lie. In this way thought patterns can be transformed.

> *"Then you will know the truth and the truth will set you free."*
> *(John 8:32)*

We must reassure those we pray for of God's unconditional love and help them to become secure.

DISCERNING SPIRITUAL ATMOSPHERES

> *"For our struggle is not against flesh and blood, but against the rulers, against the authorities, against the powers of this dark world and against the spiritual forces of evil in the heavenly realms."* *(Ephesians 6:12)*

> *"And these signs will accompany those who believe: In my name they will drive out demons..."* *(Mark 16:17)*

The battle we fight as Christians is not against flesh and blood but against principalities and powers. In those we minister to we can often see the effects of the spiritual battle:

- Depression
- Oppression
- Confusion
- Addiction such as gambling, alcoholism
- Sexual sin, affairs, divorce, illegitimacy
- Rebellion
- Blasphemy

Sometimes the signs of the grip of negative influences go back several generations and what we see is a repetitive cycle of addiction such as alcoholism, sexual or physical abuse, mental insanity or trauma, inexplicable and untimely deaths due to freak accidents, or terminal illness. Some people talk of the sense that their family is "cursed" or their home "haunted". In the church we are often good at being sympathetic listeners, pastoral counsellors or just a shoulder to cry on, but we often lack the understanding and discernment to correctly diagnose the problem and be the warriors who bring deliverance and restore peace. Jesus fully expected His disciples to rid people of their demons and bring them back into their right minds. In the same way, we are called to carry the same authority and experience the same results but we can only fight these things successfully if we know our authority in God and understand the power of the blood and name of Jesus, the Word of God and the Holy Spirit's gift of discernment.

As human beings we are created with a spirit as well as a soul and a body and yet it is the spiritual that we often overlook when we pray for healing. In the New Testament the commission to 'heal the sick' is nearly always coupled with 'and cast out demons'. Rather than see demons as a primitive and antiquated description of anything for which the known world in those days had no medical diagnosis, we must understand that the spirit realm is very real. In Africa there is a much greater appreciation of the spirit world and many in our society in the West today are all too familiar with the occult spirit world through horoscopes, tarot cards, Ouija boards and séances or witchcraft. Through often innocent exposure to these things, a door is opened to the demonic and ground is surrendered to the enemy for strongholds to form. Much of the irrational fear, nightmares and unclean thoughts with which people are plagued have roots in demonic activity, sometimes inherited from past generations.

GENERATIONAL SIN

> *"But he was pierced for our transgressions, he was crushed for our iniquities; the punishment that brought us peace was upon him, and by his wounds we are healed."* (Isaiah 53:5)

The Bible differentiates between transgressions, which are sins we commit which violate God's law, and iniquity which is a much stronger sense of an atmosphere of pervasive sin, the absence of moral or spiritual values and the presence and influence of the powers of darkness through generations. Both of these can give ground to the enemy, but while it can be easier to see a direct correlation between someone's sin or transgression and the negative influence or outcome in their life, we often underestimate or neglect the link between negative spiritual atmospheres, affliction or addictive behaviour and the generational curses whose fruit is reaped in the present. We must therefore understand that when we become Christians and are grafted into the Vine, which is Christ, we must cut ourselves off from all other spiritual inheritance and receive God's blessings in exchange for the curses. As our bloodline is cleansed through Jesus' blood, so the power of these curses is broken. Sometimes we have to help those we are praying for understand their authority in Christ and encourage them to renounce all other affiliations their family may have had in the past.

These may include:

- False religions and all other faiths which do not acknowledge Jesus as Lord
- Witchcraft and the occult
- Freemasonry and other secret societies
- Religious superstition and superstitious practices

Many of these have vows and covenants attached to them which are taken on behalf of whole families and family lines such as in the case of Freemasonry. These vows must be broken and renounced in the name of Jesus. Not until we shut the generational door can we go free.

UNDERSTANDING THE DEMONIC REALM
What do evil spirits do?
- Tempt by putting thoughts in our mind
- Deceive
- Torment and afflict
- Enslave e.g. by fear, addictions

- Compel
- Defile

How do evil spirits gain access to a person?
- Sin or rebellion which has given ground to the enemy
- Abuse and trauma
- Occult involvement
- Generational inheritance and bondage
- False religions and superstitious practices

How do we identify the need for deliverance?
- Through revelation and the gift of discernment of spirits
- Through a power encounter where the demonic manifests and is identified
- Through observing strong compulsive and destructive behaviour or torment in the person

How do we minister to people?
When we pray for people who, we suspect, are oppressed by the demonic, we need to ensure full cooperation from the person being prayed for. Demons only remain where they have legal ground and permission to stay. This does not necessarily mean that the person is responsible for the presence of the demonic but we do need to ensure that the demonic is not being, even inadvertently or ignorantly, given rights to remain. So, one area we must be sure about is that this ground is not being given over voluntarily and that the person prayed for is clear about their, and our, authority to evict the 'squatters'.

We must always preserve the dignity of the person being prayed for. This might mean that a deep prayer time is not conducted at the end of a meeting in a very public place with time pressure. It may be necessary to move someone to a side room or, if the presenting problem allows, find a more appropriate time to meet and pray.

If possible, try to have more than one person praying and ensure there is at least one person of the same sex as the person being prayed for. Remember that authority to command the demonic to go is not relative to the volume at which we pray. We do not need to shout to be confident and authoritative! It will sometimes be appropriate to get the person to pray themselves- again, we must involve the person and not forget them in the process. We need to distinguish between the person and the spirit(s) oppressing them. Sometimes they will need to repent of sin, renounce fear or unbelief or confess their own or their families' sin. Remember that the enemy is a liar and a deceiver so we need to be praying for wisdom and discernment at all times to identify the root issues.

If a spirit manifests we must remember our authority and not let noise or emotion become distracting. At times it is right to "shut down" unhelpful or distracting manifestations in order to engage and get through to the person. We need to know our limitations and always ask for more experienced help if we are out of our depth. We should always ensure after care and follow up are in place so that the person has enough support to rebuild their lives and keep the ground that has been won back from the enemy's grip. This may involve a further prayer appointment or, more often, ensuring that appropriate discipleship and healthy spiritual disciplines are in place to foster healing and restoration.

LIVING FREE – FOREVER FREE

"Finally, be strong in the Lord and in his mighty power. Put on the full armour of God so that you can take your stand against the devil's schemes. For our struggle is not against flesh and blood, but against the rulers, against the authorities, against the powers of this dark world and against the spiritual forces of evil in the heavenly realms. Therefore put on the full armour of God, so that when the day of evil comes, you may be able to stand your ground,

and after you have done everything, to stand. Stand firm then, with the belt of truth buckled around your waist, with the breastplate of righteousness in place, and with your feet fitted with the readiness that comes from the gospel of peace. In addition to all this, take up the shield of faith, with which you can extinguish all the flaming arrows of the evil one. Take the helmet of salvation and the sword of the Spirit, which is the word of God. And pray in the Spirit on all occasions with all kinds of prayers and requests. With this in mind, be alert and always keep on praying for all the saints."
(Ephesians 6:10-18)

Once we have dealt with the issues in our lives which have prevented us from living as redeemed and free children of God, we need to cultivate a lifestyle and habits which ensure that we walk out our freedom on a daily basis and defend the ground we have won back from the enemy. If we do not fill our lives with the sound of God and feed on His Word then we will soon find that the enemy is quick to fill the vacuum.

SO HOW DO WE LIVE FREE?
Fortify our minds with the Word

"The weapons we fight with are not the weapons of the world. On the contrary, they have divine power to demolish strongholds. We demolish arguments and every pretension that sets itself up against the knowledge of God, and we take captive every thought to make it obedient to Christ." (2 Corinthians 10:4-5)

As we have discussed, the mind is often the place where the heat of the battle is felt. The enemy knows that if he can fill our minds with lies, deception, doubt, unbelief and fear then our lives will begin to reflect this alternative version of reality. This means that we must learn to wash our minds with the Word of God and ensure that the truth becomes our constant diet. We need to consume the Word as medicine for our souls and learn to meditate on it daily.

While we should not dwell on the past and on our areas of battle, we need to be aware of the potential weaknesses in our defences and especially keep these fortified with the truth. So, for example, if we know we have struggled with self-esteem and feelings of unworthiness, we need to reflect on the Scriptures which speak the truth about who we are in Christ and how God sees us. This way we begin to strengthen every weak area and rid ourselves of the mindsets which have conditioned us to react out of insecurity. As we are strengthened by the truth so we learn to be those who can respond freely rather than react negatively.

> "Finally, brothers, whatever is true, whatever is noble, whatever is right, whatever is pure, whatever is lovely, whatever is admirable – if anything is excellent or praiseworthy – think about such things. Whatever you have learned or received or heard from me, or seen in me – put it into practice. And the God of peace will be with you." (Philippians 4:8-9)

We need to root out all unhelpful triggers and temptations to our thought lives. Sometimes this means that we need to be ruthless in throwing away books, videos or music which feed our thought lives in the wrong way. We cannot assume we are strong enough not to find these a temptation any longer. We need to be mindful that our minds can also be active on an unconscious or semi-conscious level and so our dreams and sleep can reflect what our minds have been fed during the day. While entrusting ourselves to the protection of God, we must be wise not to walk into the snares of the enemy voluntarily.

> "Do not conform any longer to the pattern of this world, but be transformed by the renewing of your mind. Then you will be able to test and approve what God's will is – his good, pleasing and perfect will." (Romans 12:2)

What are the weak areas in your life? What are the enemy's triggers in your life? Be aware that these can often be on an unconscious or semi-conscious level too.

Guard our hearts through worship

> "Above all else, guard your heart, for it is the wellspring of life." (Proverbs 4:23)

As well as setting our minds on godly things, we must also learn to set our affections on God through worship and prayer. Sometimes this may involve disciplining ourselves to keep Him in the number one place in our lives above the idols of money, sex and power. At other times, our hearts will need to be guarded against anger, bitterness and resentment. Every leader of significance in the Bible experienced betrayal at some time and so will we. But it was what they did with these experiences of pain and conflict which made them examples in the faith. Keeping short accounts and practising forgiveness are essential habits we must learn to cultivate in order to keep our hearts soft and open to God. It is impossible to remain a worshipper after God's own heart if our hearts become pools of bitter water so we must ask God to increase our thirst for the springs of living water which will not only refresh us but also make us givers of life to others.

We must learn to create an atmosphere of worship in our homes and find time to be in God's presence, actively seeking His face and allowing His love to immerse and transform us. As we find these "quiet times" with Him, so we will discover that we become increasingly like the One we behold.

Whenever we experience days of apparent setback where we wrestle and struggle to break through, we must remember that we have a Good Shepherd who cares for His sheep. Just because we struggle at times doesn't mean we have lost our freedom, but these days teach us to continue to allow God to heal and strengthen us to stand firm in Him.

Learn the benefits of partnership in the Body through fellowship

"And let us consider how we may spur one another on toward love and good deeds. Let us not give up meeting together, as some are in the habit of doing, but let us encourage one another – and all the more as you see the Day approaching." (Hebrews 10:24-25)

One of the key strategies of the enemy is to isolate us from the rest of the body of Christ, especially in times of struggle and battle. Jesus always gathers people and puts the lonely in families, but the enemy always scatters. Rather than suffer from the loneliness which leads us to develop complex mechanisms of self-protection, we must learn to lean into God and His family, the Church. We must retrain ourselves to be vulnerable and transparent with others so that they can help us and build us up, as well as hold us accountable, spur us on in our walk of discipleship and faith and encourage us to continue to allow God to heal and restore us. We are made for community and relationship and this is where we will thrive and grow. Where the enemy has whispered his lies and made us feel like failures, as we commit to the family of God so we begin to find our place of belonging and discover that we have gifts to offer the wider body of believers.

"Two are better than one, because they have a good return for their work: If one falls down, his friend can help him up. But pity the man who falls and has no one to help him up! Also, if two lie down together, they will keep warm. But how can one keep warm alone? Though one may be overpowered, two can defend themselves. A cord of three strands is not quickly broken." (Ecclesiastes 4:9-12)

REVERSE THE CURSE AND OPEN THE DOOR OF BLESSING

"For you were once darkness, but now you are light in the Lord. Live as children of light (for the fruit of the light consists in all goodness, righteousness and truth) and find out what pleases the

Lord. Have nothing to do with the fruitless deeds of darkness, but rather expose them." (Ephesians 5:8-11)

As we begin to live out our freedom in Christ so we find that we begin to love what God loves and hate what He hates. We also understand more of the authority we have over the principalities of darkness and learn to bring all things into the light of God. Secrets kept hidden keep us bound by guilt and shame and so have power to keep us enslaved, but there is freedom in exposing the enemy's plans and confessing the truth.

We must not be discouraged if, as part of this new walk, God reveals to us things which have been hidden such as generational sins or curses. We may find that God exposes occult or Freemasonic involvement in past generations. His intention is not to condemn us but rather to bring us into complete freedom by cleansing our bloodline and ensuring that we only pass on godly inheritance and blessing to the next generation. This is how our choices release blessing instead of curses to our children. As these things are revealed we must be prepared to seek out help or counselling for specific issues in order to truly maintain our freedom. We must also be willing to make radical changes and life choices so that no compromise remains for the enemy to gain back ground in our lives. Finally, we must understand that as children of God we are heirs of His Kingdom.

"The Spirit himself testifies with our spirit that we are God's children. Now if we are children, then we are heirs – heirs of God and co-heirs with Christ, if indeed we share in his sufferings in order that we may also share in his glory." (Romans 8:16-17)

Our destiny is to be eternally free, sharing in the glory of Christ. So we must learn to cry freedom and live forever free!

About the Author – Rachel Hickson

Rachel Hickson is an internationally respected prayer leader and Bible teacher with a recognized prophetic gift. She teaches all over the world, and is in demand as a conference speaker.

At the age of 24 Rachel, with her husband, Gordon, worked alongside Reinhard Bonnke and the Christ for All Nations team in Africa. After just six weeks in Zimbabwe she almost lost her life in a horrific car accident, but was miraculously healed by God. This incident birthed in Rachel a desire to pray and to train others to realize the full potential of a praying church.

After returning from Africa in 1990, Rachel and her husband, Gordon, pastored a group of four churches in Hertfordshire and it was during this time that they established Heartcry Ministries with the call to train and equip people to be released into effective ministries. In 2005 Rachel and Gordon moved to Oxford where Gordon was the associate minister of St. Aldates Church for six years. In 2011 he moved to become the director of Mahabba, a ministry working with Muslim communities now living in the UK, Europe and USA. They are still based in Oxford.

Rachel travels internationally, visiting Europe, North America, Africa, India and Australia. Invitations come from a variety of denominational backgrounds, both from rural and city churches. Rachel and Gordon have a passion to see cities transformed through the power of prayer and evangelism.

Rachel has been married to Gordon for over 35 years. She is the mother of two married children, Nicola and David, and has five grandchildren, Leila, Cooper, Elani, Annabelle and Jeremy.

Heartcry Ministries & Heartcry for Change Information

We work with churches and people from many nations and denominations to equip them in the following areas:

- PRAYER – Training an army of ordinary people in prayer schools and seminars to become confident to break the sound barrier and pray informed, intelligent and passionate prayers.

- PROPHETIC – Equipping the Church to be an accurate prophetic voice in the nation by teaching in training schools and conferences the principles of the prophetic gift. We seek to train people who are passionate to know the presence of God, are available to hear His voice and then learn to speak His word with accuracy so that lives can be touched and changed.

- WOMEN – Delivering a message of hope to women across the nations and cultures to help them arise with a new confidence so that they can be equipped and ready to fulfil their destiny and execute their Kingdom purpose.

- CAPITAL CITIES – Standing in the capital cities of the world, working with government institutions, businesses and the Church and then crying out for a new alignment of the natural and spiritual government in these places. A cry for London and beyond.

- BUSINESS & FINANCE – Connecting business people with their Kingdom purpose so that provision can partner more effectively with vision and accelerate the purpose of God in nations. Connecting commerce, community and church for change!

- LEADERS OF TOMORROW – Mentoring and encouraging younger leaders to pioneer the next move of God in the areas of politics and government, social action and justice issues, creative arts, media and the ministry.

- NATIONS – Partnering with nations in Africa, the Middle East and India by supplying teaching, training and practical resources to strengthen and resource them as they work for breakthrough in their nations.

- MEDIA, TV & SATELLITE – Developing training materials to equip and disciple the Church in the nations to understand and fulfil their responsibility. To be a voice of encouragement through TV into the homes of the army of ordinary people praying for impossible situations.

- RESOURCES & CONFERENCES – Writing books, manuals and training materials that will equip the Church to be prepared. Running conferences and training days where leaders and the church can be encouraged to continue in their purpose and calling.

Heartcry hopes to continue strengthening the Church to connect with their community whilst encouraging the people to hear the urgent call to prayer. Now is the time to pray and cry out for our land and continent and watch what God will do for us!

HEARTCRY MINISTRIES
P.O. Box 737
Oxford, Oxon
OX1 9FA UK
www.heartcry.co.uk

HEARTCRY FOR CHANGE USA
P.O. Box 2354
Kirkland
WA 98083 USA
www.heartcryforchange.com

FOLLOW RACHEL AND THE TEAM ON FACEBOOK
www.facebook.com/Heartcryforchange/

Other Books by Rachel Hickson

Release My Frozen Assets
A look at the role of women in the church

EAT THE WORD SPEAK THE WORD

Run Your Race
SOMETHING TO LIVE FOR!

Pathway of Peace
A 40 DAY DEVOTIONAL

STEPPING STONES TO FREEDOM
A 40 DAY DEVOTIONAL

Visit our online shop for great deals on books, ebooks, audiobooks and more.

www.heartcryforchange.com/shop